Islamic States in Conflict

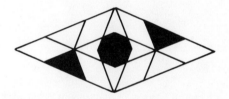

William Spencer

FRANKLIN WATTS
NEW YORK | LONDON
TORONTO | SYDNEY | 1983
AN IMPACT BOOK

Map courtesy of Vantage Art, Inc.

Library of Congress Cataloging in Publication Data

Spencer, Wiliam.
Islamic states in conflict.

(An Impact book)
Bibliography: p.
Includes index.
Summary: Describes the history of conflict
among Middle Eastern tribes and nations
before and since the birth of Islam.
1. Near East—History—Juvenile literature.
[1. Near East—History] I. Title.
DS62.S65   1983   956   82-20125
ISBN 0-531-04544-7

Contents

And We make [this scripture] easy in
    thy tongue [O Muhammad]
Only that thou mayst bear good tidings
    therewith
Unto those who ward off [evil],
And warn therewith the froward folk.

And how many a generation before them
    have we destroyed!
Canst thou [Muhammad] see a single man
    of them,
Or hear from them the slightest sound.

Koran 61: 97, 98

To those countless generations
and to my wife,
Elizabeth, of this generation,
who has helped beyond measure
to bring it forth!

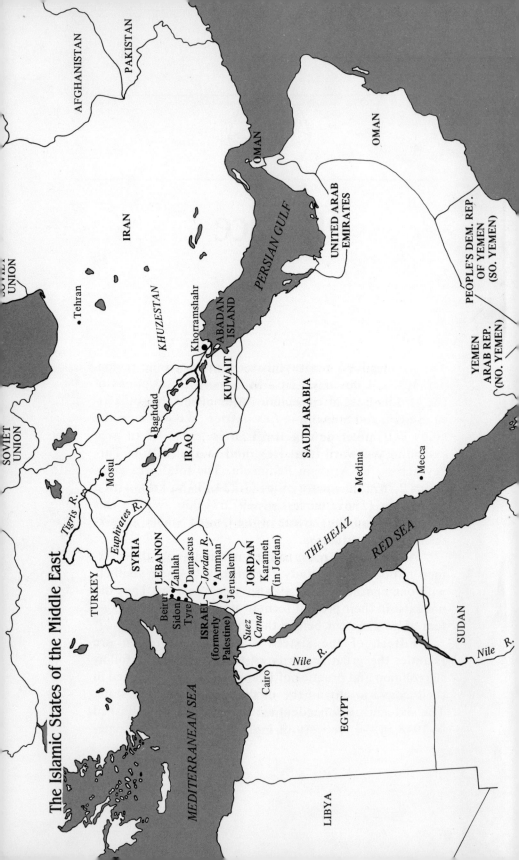

The Islamic States of the Middle East

AFGHANISTAN

PAKISTAN

SOVIET UNION

SOVIET UNION

IRAN

• Tehran

KHUZESTAN

Khorramshahr •

ABADAN ISLAND

KUWAIT

Baghdad •

IRAQ

Mosul •

Tigris R.

Euphrates R.

TURKEY

SYRIA

LEBANON

Beirut •
Sidon •
Tyre •
Zahlah •
Damascus •
Jordan R.
Amman •

ISRAEL
(formerly
Palestine)

Jerusalem •

JORDAN

Karameh
(in Jordan)

*Suez
Canal*

Cairo •

MEDITERRANEAN SEA

EGYPT

LIBYA

Nile R.

SUDAN

Nile R.

THE HEJAZ

RED SEA

SAUDI ARABIA

• Medina

• Mecca

PERSIAN GULF

OMAN

OMAN

UNITED ARAB EMIRATES

PEOPLE'S DEM. REP.
OF YEMEN
(SO. YEMEN)

YEMEN
ARAB REP.
(NO. YEMEN)

Preface

The Middle East geographically is an indefinite region, perhaps best described as a subregion. Descriptions of the Middle East often include Afghanistan, North Africa, Sudan, and Somalia in East Africa. We will limit the study of conflict among the Islamic states to an area extending eastward from Iran, and southeast from Turkey across the Arabian Peninsula. The total area comprises 2,789,262 square miles (7,224,189 sq km), with a population (1981 figures) of 197,671,000. Within this area, three-fourths the size of the United States, are sixteen sovereign states.

An important point to keep in mind about these sixteen nations as we study the history of their conflicts with one another is that all are "new" nations. They did not exist in their present form or under their present system of government before the end of World War II.

Fifteen of the sixteen states in the region are Islamic; the great majority of their populations follow the religion and practice of Islam, which is established in their constitutions as the official religion of the state. The sixteenth independent state, Israel, was established in 1948 in the territory of Palestine as a Jewish homeland. The Arab-Israeli and Israeli-Palestinian conflicts are outside the scope of this book, but they are important factors in the tensions and rivalries of the Islamic states.

A final point about relations among the Middle East's Islamic states has to do with ethnic differences. Two of these states, Turkey and Iran, are non-Arab. One, Lebanon, is half Christian, half Arab in population. The rest are Arab/Islamic. Turkey, which controlled most of the region as the Ottoman (Islamic) Empire for centuries, became a republic, much reduced in size, in the 1920s and formally renounced any interference in the affairs of its neighbors. Thus Turkey has not been a factor in Islamic state conflict since that time. Iran, also an ancient empire, had a constitutional monarchy from the early 1900s until 1978, but for reasons that will be explained in the book, has not renounced conflict with its Arab neighbors. The Arab states, although linked by language, religion, and culture, have not as yet been able to resolve natural rivalries, even though they are committed in principle to the establishment of a single Arab nation.

Despite their many differences, the Islamic states are united in their common need to establish themselves as truly independent nations, free from foreign influence in their affairs. They are also united in their attempts to find ways to adapt their religious values to sudden wealth and technology in the twentieth century.

1

Weight of the Past

Conflict is an old, old story in the region known today as the Middle East. Long before the religion of Islam was founded in the seventh century A.D., Middle Eastern peoples were warring with each other, glaring suspiciously at their neighbors or waiting, weapons in hand, behind the walls of their cities for attack by an invader. More often than not the enemy was a relative. Four thousand years ago a poet at the pharaoh's court in Egypt wrote sadly,

> *To whom can I speak today?*
> *Brothers are evil*
> *And the friends of today unlovable.*

In the area where today the armies of Iran and Iraq, "brother" Islamic nations, battle each other with missiles, jet planes and artillery, a tablet was found recording the victory of Yakhdun-Lim, ruler of the city of Mari, over an army from a nearby city, thirty-eight centuries ago: "I, Yakhdun-Lim, powerful king, wild ox in strength and valor, with the help of the sun-god Shamash, have defended the city from our enemy and driven them away." It seems that ever since then, down through history, the Middle East's peoples have been battling over land, livestock, women, water rights, the favor of the gods, or any one of a dozen other reasons. The weapons of today may be different and more destructive, but the results in terms of human suffering and property damage are just as tragic.

Why has conflict been so central a factor in Middle Eastern history both before and after the rise of Islam? One reason is the way Middle Eastern life was organized under governments and laws. The world's earliest cities developed in the Middle East and as they grew there was fierce competition among them for land and economic resources. About the time our unknown Egyptian poet was complaining about false friendships, Hammurabi, the sixth king of the first dynasty of the city-state of Babylon, was busy drawing up a code of laws for his people. The Code of Hammurabi helped to make Babylon into the most efficient and powerful city-state in the Middle East. It dominated its neighbors and acquired so much wealth that it was one of the wonders of the ancient world.

A basic principle of Hammurabi's Code is the *lex talionis*, translated as "an eye for an eye, a tooth for a tooth"—in other words, punishment to fit the crime, and compensation to the victim equal to the loss or damage or injury sustained. As an example, Hammurabi's law governing theft might specify that a thief caught stealing would have his right hand cut off, that being the hand that did the stealing. The *lex talionis* principle spread throughout the region as Hammurabi's Code was copied by other city-states or imposed by the Babylonians upon conquered peoples. One of these conquered peoples was the Hebrews, who already worshiped a stern, vengeful but just god named Yahweh (or Jehovah). The *lex talionis* seemed appropriate to the Hebrew religion, Judaism, and it was not until Jesus Christ came along to urge people to "love thy neighbor" and "turn the other

(4)

cheek" that the doctrine of forgiveness and tolerance associated primarily with Christianity became widespread. Centuries later when Islam developed, its laws and practices were closer to Judaism than to Christianity. Like Yahweh, the God of Islam (Allah) is stern and vengeful, although just, and Allah's laws prescribe revenge. Only Allah can forgive!

The *lex talionis* is only part of the explanation for the long history and persistence of conflict in the Middle East. Until very recently when mankind acquired some control over the earth's environment, human behavior was shaped by that environment. Eskimos live in a particular way because of the environment they inhabit; so do the Bushmen of the Kalahari Desert of South Africa and the Indians of tropical Brazil. The Middle Eastern environment is a harsh one. There are great differences in climate and widely scattered areas of fertile land where people can grow enough crops to feed themselves. Modern technology has not entirely changed the appearance of the landscape. Pilgrims going to Mecca, the holy city of Islam, from Jiddah, on the Red Sea coast of Arabia, now travel by a macadam road, but the desert on each side of the road is just as bare and stony as it was fourteen hundred years ago when Islam was founded as a religion. As another example, from the peak of Mount Nebo in Jordan, where God showed Moses (*Deuteronomy* 34:1–3) the Promised Land—"All the land of Gilead, unto Dan, . . . and all the land of Judah unto the utmost sea, and the south, and the plain of the valley of Jericho, the city of palm trees, unto Zoar"—there is nothing but a wilderness of barren hills stretching as far as the horizon. Yet just beyond the horizon, where the muddy Jordan River empties into the Dead Sea, are the lush irrigated farms and modern cities of Israel.

Unlike other regions of the world, the Middle East has such a difference between desert and cultivated areas that there is a special word for the latter—the word "oa-

(5)

sis." It describes a place where there is enough underground water and fertile soil to support a permanent village population. The large city of Damascus (with a population of over one million), the capital of Syria, is actually an oasis in the Syrian desert watered by underground springs and the Barada River. An oasis has a kind of magic feeling about it. When you arrive there, usually after many hours of travel, it is as if you had stumbled into a paradise of palm trees and gardens that is totally different from the barren countryside around it.

The desert-oasis relationship was one of the historical conditions necessary for Middle Eastern conflict to develop. Biologists might call this relationship a *symbiosis*, what the dictionary defines as "the close association of two or more different organisms which may be, but is not necessarily, of benefit to each." The people who lived in an oasis and the nomads, or bedouin, of the desert had this kind of relationship with each other. The bedouin brought their livestock—horses, camels and sometimes sheep and cattle to the oasis to barter or sell in order to buy the things they needed to survive in the desert— flour, sugar, salt, coffee, cloth, weapons. The oasis people produced these things, plus food crops for their own use, but there was not enough arable land or water around the oasis for livestock-raising.

Conflict developed when, for example, there were long periods of drought in the desert areas and the bedouin were forced to move into, or near, the oases, making extra demands on the water and food supply. Out in the desert, the various bedouin tribes often clashed over rights to water-wells or the few grazing lands. Sometimes members of one tribe would kidnap girls from another tribe as brides for their warriors. Such actions would set off a chain reaction of raids called *ghazus*, which were a common feature of life in the desert.

A second historical condition for Middle Eastern conflict is the mountaineer-lowlander relationship. The

(6)

region has a number of high, rugged mountain ranges such as the Elburz mountains in Iran and the Taurus in Turkey. From time immemorial mountains offered refuge to peoples escaping from war, religious persecution or cruel governments in the cities and towns of the lowlands. Even today there are pockets of religious, ethnic or language groups scattered throughout the Middle Eastern mountain ranges. These mountain clans are suspicious of all outsiders and reject the authority of whatever government is in power in the lowlands.

Examples of mountain peoples who behave in this way are the Maronites and the Kurds. The Maronites, a Christian sect, took refuge in the mountains of Lebanon many centuries ago to escape persecution by the armies of the Greek Orthodox Christian government of the Byzantine Empire. The Muslims left them alone. Eventually, with foreign help, they organized the modern Republic of Lebanon, "a Christian island in a Muslim sea." The Maronites say that they are the rulers of Lebanon, and this attitude has brought them into conflict with their Muslim neighbors.

The Kurds are a mountain people around whom conflict has swirled ever since they appeared in history. They claim to be descended from the ancient Assyrians. The Assyrians were always coming down from the mountains to attack the lowland cities, and the modern Kurds are just as warlike. But the Kurds are not interested in conquest. All they want is independence in their own mountain country, which they call Kurdistan. Unfortunately, Kurdistan today is not a country, it is an ideal. The Kurds live scattered across the mountains of four Middle Eastern countries—Iran, Iraq, Syria and Turkey. These countries spend much of their time, money and military power trying to make the Kurds submit to government control.

The position of the Kurds is different in each country. Turkey pretends that the Kurds in its territory do not exist, calling them "Eastern Turks" or "Mountain Turks." In 1946 and again during the 1979–80 revolution in Iran, the Kurds tried to set up a self-governing province in Iran. The Arab government of Iraq has been trying for years to put down a rebellion in Iraqi Kurdistan. Except for their religion, the Kurds have little in common with the Iranians, Turks or Arabs who rule them. The Kurds have their own language, literature, customs, and ancestral links, all of which make them different from their lowland neighbors.

Like the desert bedouin, however, the Kurds spend as much of their time fighting each other as they do fighting government forces. There is an old proverb in the Middle East which goes as follows:

I against my brother
My brother and I against my cousin
My brother, my cousin and I against the world.

Although in our modern world it is more likely to be nations rather than individuals or groups within nations that engage in war, conflict in the Middle East very often comes about because of the clash of Arab, Kurdish, Turkish or other "brothers" with each other.

Conflict in Arabia, the boot-shaped peninsula which is the home of the Arabs and the birthplace of Islam, developed naturally from the desert-oasis and mountain-lowland relationship of its peoples. The peninsula is large, over one million square miles in area (almost four times the size of Texas). It is divided into a number of separate environmental sub-regions. Until recently, before the development of modern airplanes and paved roads, the peoples of these sub-regions had little contact with each other. Except in Yemen in the southwest corner of the peninsula—where there was dependable rainfall and high mountains to keep invaders out—life in Arabia was precarious at best. Bedouin tribes roamed the vast deserts, going from well to well, pasturing their flocks in the few areas where there was enough vegetation.

We have already described some of the reasons why conflict was part of the normal way of life for these bedouin. Often disputes would lead to conflict which became, in time, a blood feud between clans or whole tribes, feuds which could go on so long that everyone forgot their origins. One such feud began when a man from one nomadic clan accidentally cut a boy from another tribe with a knife; both clans had stopped at the same well for water and the boy was watching the man whittle a block of wood. The boy ran to his family's tent and said the cut was intentional. His relative went to the whittler to claim damages. There was a heated argument that turned to violence. Many people were injured on both sides, and from that day on the two clans became bitter enemies, all over a trifling knife wound.

This incident shows us certain aspects of Arab character that contributed to their sense of conflict as natural and expected behavior. One aspect is that of pride. Arabs have traditionally rejected any higher authority over themselves except that of the clan. Power, strength and safety for the individual have rested in the clan.

A second aspect of Arab character relevant to conflict is that of a sense of equality. Every tribe, every clan, feels itself equal to every other clan or tribe. In the past, when there were disputes between clans (such as a blood feud), it was difficult for arbitrators to settle them if called in from a third clan, because neither party to the dispute would accept the views of the other about the problem involved. The only time Arabian clans or tribes united was as a last resort against invaders from the outside.

This sense of equality has continued up to the present day. When the Imam (ruler) of Yemen was overthrown by a military coup in 1955, civil war broke out between the mountain tribes, who supported him, and the tribes of the lowland coastal plain, who had opposed his cruel regime. But when Egyptian troops were sent to Yemen to help the lowland tribes, many of them saw the Egyptians not as helpers but as invaders, and joined the mountain tribes who were fighting them.

Historically, conflict in Arabia was somewhat more extreme than in other parts of the Middle East, being an integral part of Arabian life. There is, however, one other element in Middle Eastern life that is very strong among the Arabs and has contributed to their tendency to conflict. This is the element of predestined fate.

Long before Islam developed in Arabia, Arabs believed that some powerful force in the universe decided on the shape and form of each person's life—in other words, one's destiny. They believed that four things were decided before each person's birth: its sex, whether or not it would eat well, whether its life would be wretched or happy and its term of life. In Arabia, therefore, one's food, fortune and life span depended upon factors beyond one's control. They could not be changed by any action or choice on any person's part. This idea of a powerful force directing human destinies was incorporated into Islam as the idea of *Kismet*, meaning Fate. An old desert story tells of a starving man, lying by a road, who sees a trader and his wife riding along on their camels. The man leaps on the stranger, robs him of wife and camels and leaves him by the side of the road. Neither man thinks of the action as cruel, wrong or unjust. It is Fate that has given each of them good fortune or bad luck.

In the next two chapters we will describe the new religion of Islam, how it developed in Arabia, and what changes it brought to the way of life of the Arabs and then other Middle Eastern peoples. Islam brought a completely new set of beliefs and obligations to the Arabs. It substituted obedience to the power and authority of One God for the traditional Arab obedience to the power and authority of the clan or tribe. Gradually the Arabs, and

(10)

then other Middle Eastern peoples like the Turks and Iranians, became members of a single "community of believers," equal under God and obedient to God. But the old notion of the equality of clans and tribes has continued up to the present day. When the king of Saudi Arabia holds a public meeting every day to receive complaints and hear requests from Saudi citizens, he is observing a tradition that goes back into the dim past, and every citizen who presents a complaint or a request feels in his heart that he is just as good as the king.

2

Islam, a "Conflict" Religion

As we said in the previous chapter, conflict has been an intrinsic part of Middle Eastern life since the start of recorded history in the region. It was a result in part of the fragmented nature of Middle Eastern society, divided into rival clans and tribes. From time to time, one tribe or group of tribes gained enough power over others to be able to establish control over large territories. Babylon was able to do so, and after Babylon came the Persian (Iranian) Empire, which lasted about two hundred years. Much later, the Romans ruled the western half of the Middle East, and the successors to the first Persian emperors, the Sassanids, ruled the eastern half. The boundary between these two empires was the Euphrates River, in what is today Iraq. When the Roman Empire collapsed, in the fifth century A.D., its Middle Eastern provinces became part of the Christian Greek Byzantine Empire. The eastern part of the region continued under the rule of the Sassanids. The two empires fought each other constantly, because each one thought it had the "true" religion which should be followed by all peoples—the Greeks having the "correct" form of Christianity, the Sassanids having a religion of

(12)

two forces, Good (Light) and Evil (Darkness) which rule the universe. As you can see, wars over religion go back a very long time in history.

The tribes of Arabia were hardly ever involved in this conflict. They were peripheral to the action, and were not under the control of either empire. In fact, there was only one region of Arabia that had much contact at all with the outside world. This was the region called the Hejaz. It was an important region to the world trade of the time, because major north-south and east-west trade routes passed through it. Camel caravans carried the spices, silks, ivory, gold, precious gems and other goods from India and the Far East, northward through the Hejaz to the markets of the great cities of the two empires. The journey was a long one through barren country, and the few water wells were convenient stopping places for the weary caravans. Small permanent settlements grew up gradually around these wells.

The most important of these Hejaz settlements was Mecca. It developed because it was located at the center of the main north-south and east-west caravan routes. The merchants of Mecca took full advantage of their location, providing comfortable beds, food, stables for the camels and other services. In return, they could count on a 100-percent profit on their investments in underwriting the camel caravans.

There was another reason for Mecca's importance. Its principal well, Zam Zam, was 140 feet deep, with crystal-clear water. Zam Zam water was believed to cure all kinds of illnesses, and people came from near and far to drink from it.

Near the well was a large rock, different from other rocks in the area because it was ebony black and shiny. No one knew how it got there and the people who came to the well, not to mention the caravans, were afraid of it because it was so unusual. (It was probably an ancient meteorite.) Visitors to Mecca thought it had magic pow-

(13)

ers and worshiped it. The citizens of Mecca decided to capitalize on the rock's appeal. They built a cube-shaped stone hut called the *Ka'ba* ("Cube" in Arabic) around the Black Stone and charged fees to visitors who wanted to kiss it for good luck. Visitors to Mecca were made to understand that they were in a sacred place where all forms of conflict were prohibited.

Gradually, Mecca became a pilgrimage center. Once a year pilgrims came by the thousands to drink the waters of Zam Zam, kiss the Black Stone, and worship at the shrines of gods and goddesses placed around the Ka'ba by the city fathers. The Ka'ba itself was eventually enlarged into a stone building.

This pilgrim trade was very lucrative and made Mecca rich. By the middle of the fifth century A.D., one tribe, the Quraysh (named after an ancestor) had become the dominant group in Mecca, and its senior members took care of arrangements for pilgrims. We would call the Quraysh an elite—a merchant aristocracy, though not all of its families enjoyed the same prosperity.

MUHAMMAD, MESSENGER OF GOD

One day in the year A.D. 570 a boy was born into one of the poorer clans of the Quraysh, a family whose only importance was that the boy's grandfather had been keeper of the keys to the Ka'ba. The boy was given the name Muhammad, meaning "the praised one." He had a difficult childhood, with no indication from his early life that he would become the founder of a new religion which, in our day, includes 800 million members.

Muhammad was orphaned at the age of six, and apparently went to work as a stable boy at the age of ten. We hear no more about him until the age of twenty-five. By then, surprisingly, Muhammad had overcome his handicaps. Somewhere along the line he became the business agent of a well-to-do widow who had invested

(14)

her late husband's money in the caravan trade. She and Muhammad were married when he was twenty-five and she was forty. Muhammad settled down to become one of Mecca's business leaders, known especially for his ability to settle disputes.

We know nothing about Muhammad's life for the next fifteen years. But when he was forty he had a strange experience. It was his habit to go out of his house in the evening and walk up to a cave in the hills above Mecca, where he would sit and meditate.

One night in the year A.D. 610, Muhammad heard a loud voice speaking to him in the cave. Terrified, he rushed home and asked his wife to cover him with blankets, as he was shivering with cold. Then he heard the voice again. The voice told him that he had been chosen as a Messenger of God, who was to bring his own people, the Arabs, to believe in One God, an all-powerful God who knew all things and held power over all people as well as the universe. The voice then cried out to Muhammad: "You, wrapped in your mantle, arise and warn!"

This was the first of many revelations sent by God to Muhammad. The businessman of Mecca did not know why, but for some reason he had been chosen to bring the Word of God to his people, and after them to other peoples. Other peoples, Christians and Jews, also had a belief in One God; Muhammad probably knew this from his travels. But they had strayed from the true faith. They needed to be shown the way back to worship of God. As for the Arabs, they worshiped only inanimate objects and the forces of nature—the rain, the wind, the sun. Worship of God would bring them together as a people and give them pride in a religion of their own.

From then on Muhammad was a changed person. He went about Mecca preaching belief in God (Allah, in Arabic) to the exclusion of all other gods. Those who accepted him became members of his new religion. Its name was, and is, *Islam*, an Arabic word meaning "submission." Those who submit to Allah and His Word as

(15)

revealed to Muhammad and written down in the Koran (in Arabic, Qur'an), the "Bible" of Islam, are called Muslims.

Muhammad's preaching soon led to conflict with the leaders of Mecca. They saw that if enough people became Muslims their pilgrimage business would be ruined. They sent thugs to break up his street-corner sermons, called him a liar, a fraud, a false prophet. His followers were threatened, beaten up, and the shops would not sell them food. A wall of silence greeted Muhammad when he went about Mecca. Only the protection of his clan saved Muhammad from personal danger.

By 622 A.D. the prospects for Muhammad and his new religion were bleak. He still had only a few followers, perhaps two hundred in all. Worse yet, he was no longer under the protection of his clan because his uncle, the head of the clan, had died, and threats were made on his life. Then a delegation from another city came to see him. There was a dispute between factions in that city. The delegation asked Muhammad to come and settle the dispute. In return he and his followers would be protected from their enemies in Mecca, and they could stay as long as they liked.

Muhammad agreed to the terms. The Muslims began leaving Mecca quietly in small groups. Muhammad and his son-in-law Ali were the last to leave. They left just ahead of a "death squad" that had come to Muhammad's house. The people of the new city welcomed the Muslims. When Muhammad settled their dispute they gave their city a new name in his honor, Medinat-Nabi, "City of the Prophet," usually shortened to Medina. The citizens submitted to Islam en masse, and helped Muhammad with his plans to overcome the leaders of Mecca and establish Islam as the religion of his people.

Conflict between Mecca and the Muslims became open warfare with Muslim raiding parties attacking the caravans going to and from Mecca. One of these raids led to a battle with the armed escorts sent along to protect the caravans. The Muslims were outnumbered eight to one, but they fought like lions, fired up by their belief in Allah. Even if they were killed, Muhammad assured them they would go straight to Paradise. The Muslims routed their enemies and captured enough booty from the caravan to last them for months.

The war between the Muslims and Mecca went on for eight years until the leaders of Mecca gave up, discouraged by losses in manpower and a shut-down of the pilgrimage business. They accepted Muhammad's leadership and submitted to Islam. In 630 A.D. the Messenger of God returned to his hometown at the head of a thousand followers. He said that henceforth only Allah would be worshiped in Mecca. The Ka'ba became Allah's House of Worship, the center of the annual pilgrimage of Muslims to Mecca which Muhammad continued from the previous pilgrimage tradition.

For the next two years tribal delegations came to Muhammad from all over Arabia to submit to Islam, and for the first time in their history there was peace among the tribes. Muhammad continued to receive revelations from Allah. These were first memorized, but later they were written down as the Koran, the Holy Book of Islam. Every message that Allah sent to people through Muhammad is included in the Koran. Muslims believe, therefore, that the Koran is the literal word of Allah. It tells them everything they need to know in order to live their lives in accordance with Allah's wishes.

In 632 A.D. Muhammad led the annual pilgrimage to Mecca to worship at the Ka'ba. It had become his custom to give a sermon during the formal religious services held on Fridays. Muhammad told his followers:

Hear my words O Muslims and take them to heart. Know ye that every Muslim is a brother unto every other Muslim and that ye are one

(17)

*brotherhood. It is not lawful for any one of you
to take unto himself anything that belongs to a
brother unless it is willingly given to him by
that brother.*

It is important to understand that this plea for peace and
brotherhood among Muslims came from Muhammad's
interpretation of Allah's wishes. Because Muslims after
his time failed to live up to his ideals does not change the
fact that the Messenger of Allah sought peace, rather
than the sword.

Several months later Muhammad fell ill, complaining of headaches and high fever. As the women of his
household bathed his forehead with cool water, he mut-
tered a few prayers, lapsed into unconsciousness and
died. He was sixty-two years old.

What had Muhammad accomplished in his relatively short lifetime? First, he had united his people, the
Arabs, for the first time in their history. He had given
them a simple faith, one based on direct communication
with Allah, and available to them for all time in the
Koran. Secondly, his own life became a model for Muslims of future generations. Muhammad's own decisions
about his behavior and the behavior of his followers,
called Hadith ("Traditions") are second only to the
Koran as guidance for the Muslim community. Thirdly,
Muhammad, on the basis of revelations, defined certain
requirements for the practice of Islam, called the "Five
Pillars" because they "support" the House of Islam. The
Five Pillars are: (1) the confession of faith—in Allah,
and in Muhammad as the Messenger of Allah; (2)
prayer, required five times daily; (3) fasting for the
entire lunar month of Ramadan, the month when
Muhammad received his first revelations; (4) alms-giv-
ing, which includes tithing, aid to the poor and in modern
times taxes for social services; and (5) pilgrimage, which
is to be made at least once in one's lifetime, to the holy
cities of Mecca and Medina.

(18)

MUHAMMAD'S SUCCESSORS

The news of Muhammad's death spread rapidly to the far corners of Arabia. The people closest to him—his family, the companions who had followed him from the beginning of his ministry, the Muslims of Medina—could not believe it at first. They had come to believe him immortal, the most perfect of men. In this emergency the Muslims turned back to Arab tribal custom. The tribe's elders had always made decisions for the group—whether to raid, to fight, to move or not—and elected one of their number as the head chief of the tribe. Now the senior leaders of the Muslims talked in low tones. They had to make a quick decision. No time could be lost because Muhammad left no instructions about a successor and the Muslim community could easily fall apart.

The senior leaders elected their oldest member, Abu Bakr, as the leader of the Muslim community. Abu Bakr was the logical choice. He was the oldest—therefore, according to them, the wisest. He had been, also, the second convert to Islam after Muhammad's wife. Abu Bakr's title would be *caliph*, establishing the title for all successors of Muhammad until the last caliph was deposed in 1924. Although the majority of Muslims readily accepted Abu Bakr as the successor to Muhammad, a minority did not, with important consequences for conflict in Islam.

Abu Bakr died after serving as caliph for only two years. After a series of successors a caliph named Uthman was murdered by the minority which originally opposed Abu Bakr. It called itself the Shia. Uthman was murdered because the Shia felt Ali, Muhammad's adopted son and first cousin, should have been caliph. Ali was also the father of Muhammad's two surviving grandsons, Hassan and Hussein. Ali became caliph after Uthman's murder, but after a short time he too was murdered. The murder of Ali set off a power struggle between the Shia and the Sunni (who form the majority of Muslims) that has continued to the present.

(19)

THE SHIA IMAMS

The main difference between Sunni and Shia grew out of this conflict over the office of caliph. The Sunni believed that the office, although an important one, could be filled by any qualified Muslim. However, the Shia belief in the right of Muhammad's direct descendants to lead the Islamic community led them to have a special reverence for the wisdom, divine insight and prophetic powers of Muhammad's descendants through Ali, whom they call Imams. Between 661 and 878 A.D. there were twelve Imams, Ali being considered the first, his sons Hassan and Hussein the second and third and thereafter the eldest male descendant of Hussein in each generation.

The line of Imams came to an abrupt end in 878 A.D. The son of the eleventh Imam was only twelve years old when his father died. One morning twelve-year-old Muhammad disappeared into the narrow streets of the city where he lived. He was never seen again by his family or by anyone else. Because the twelfth Imam was the last surviving male in the line, his disappearance left the Shia in a quandary. Would they finally have to accept the authority of the caliphs? Some Shia leaders thought otherwise. They said the twelfth Imam could not possibly be dead. God had raised him up and hidden him somewhere between heaven and earth. When God was ready he would allow the Imam to return to earth, announce the Day of Judgment, and give the faithful Shia their just reward in Paradise. Until that time came, the Shia should obey the orders of their religious leaders who were acting on behalf of the twelfth Imam.

By acting on behalf of the twelfth Imam the Shia religious leaders gained control over the Shia community. They have kept this control ever since despite many changes of government in Islamic lands. There are no basic differences in belief, ritual or requirements between Sunni and Shia, although they tend to live in separate communities. Except in Iran, which is 95 per-

(20)

cent Shia, the Shia are a minority in the Islamic world and are found primarily in Iraq, Syria, Lebanon and the countries of the Arabian Peninsula.

Particularly in Iran, the Shia developed a hierarchy among religious leaders based on wisdom and assumed divine insight. The wisest and most divinely inspired leaders were called the ayatollahs. Shia religious leaders have kept the tradition of the "hidden" twelfth Imam alive up to the present day. This religious power has enabled them to play an important role in Iran—a role that produced in 1979 the Islamic Republic of Iran, dominated by Ayatollah Rouhollah Khomeini.

THE PRINCIPLE OF JIHAD

At the beginning of this chapter we described Islam as "a conflict religion." There is a basic principle in Islam which has had a great deal to do with conflict within the religion. It is the principle of *jihad*, "holy struggle." It is one of Allah's revelations in the Koran, which means that the Muslim must obey it. Jihad is often translated "holy war," but the better term is "struggle," because the Koran tells Muslims that they must not only struggle against the enemies of Islam outside its territory, but also against unjust or corrupt leaders within. Along with these struggles there is an element in jihad of struggle against one's own sins and weaknesses. Because jihad affects so many aspects of Muslim behavior—personal behavior, the behavior of leaders, the behavior of Islamic nations toward each other and the outside world—it is often referred to as the Sixth Pillar of Islam.

Both Sunni and Shia believe in jihad, the Shia somewhat more strongly because their minority status and historical experience have given them a sense of martyrdom. One particular Shia group used to send its members in secret to try to kill leaders who had been particularly cruel to the people under their authority. Drugged with hashish and fired by conviction they were doing right to rid the Islamic world of unjust leaders, these men were known as the Hashishin, from which we get the English word "assassins." They were not always successful, and even if they succeeded, they were often killed on the spot. But either way the Hashishin were convinced that they would go straight to Paradise because their cause was just. The shah of Iran and President Anwar al-Sadat of Egypt are recent additions to a long list of Islamic rulers and officials who have been killed or removed from office for allegedly ruling "unjustly."

During the first six centuries of the caliphate (632-1258 A.D.) there were various internal conflicts within the lands of Islam. The only time Muslims put aside their differences to any concerted extent was during the Crusades (1100–1300 A.D.). An army of European Christian knights captured Jerusalem in 1099 and set up a Kingdom of Jerusalem in the Holy Land. Muslim leaders called for a jihad against the Crusaders, and volunteers came from the far corners of the caliphate to fight the infidels. A Kurdish general, Saladin, recaptured Jerusalem in 1187, and the last Crusader stronghold, Acre, fell in 1291.

But the unity of Islam was brief; it needed an outside enemy to hold it together. The closest Muslims came to establishing a unified Islamic state, in the modern, European sense of the term, was the Ottoman Turkish Empire, which will be discussed in the next chapter. Even this state, whose ruler, the sultan, declared himself also to be caliph, did not control all Muslims. He particularly did not control Shia Iran, and the Ottoman sultans spent a good deal of time in jihad against their Iranian rivals.

3

The Rise
and Fall of
Islam

After Muhammad's death most of the Arabian tribes
that had pledged allegiance to him reneged on their
pledge. They had to be reconverted to Islam by forceful
persuasion. Yet within twenty years, Muslim armies
sweeping out of Arabia had overcome the Persian king,
defeated the Byzantines and taken much of their territory in the Middle East, conquered Egypt and much of
North Africa. A century after the death of the Messenger of Allah, the green banner of Islam fluttered over a
vast region, from Spain and Morocco on the Atlantic
Ocean eastward to the borders of China and deep into
Africa. Muslim missionaries brought the new religion by
ship to India, the East Indies, Malaya and Singapore.

Why did Islam spread so rapidly in such a short
time? One reason for its spread was that it had very simple requirements. But there were also some practical reasons for its success. It gave poor, uneducated or landless
people a chance to rise to high rank or acquire great
wealth through service with the caliphs. Advancement,
in the Islamic community, was based on ability—not
"who you know" but "what you know."

Also, because Arabic was the language of Islam, it
served as a bond to unite peoples from different back-

grounds. It was the language of Islamic government, business and finance, trade and education; to improve their position the Muslims had to learn it.

Another point in Islam's favor was its tolerance and respect for other religions, at least those that believed in one God and had their own sacred books or scriptures. Thus Christians and Jews were allowed to practice their own forms of worship without interference. Although these non-Muslim minorities were occasionally mistreated or persecuted, in general they fared very well in the lands of the caliph. In some areas, such as Spain, local rulers depended on Christians and Jews for certain functions, appointing them to positions of trust, and in Egypt the Christian Coptic community provided Muslim governors with tax collectors, bookkeepers, scribes and accountants.

As we said in Chapter 2, during the first years of the caliphate (632–1258 A.D.) there was periodic conflict between local Muslim rulers and instability in some areas where ineffective governors failed to maintain law and order. From time to time the caliphs went to war with the Byzantine Empire or during the Crusades with European Christian powers. But there was also a great deal of peaceful development. Islam placed a high value on learning, particularly in philosophy and the natural sciences, mathematics, astronomy and geography. Muslims prided themselves on being the heirs to Greek and Latin civilization, translating works of ancient scholars into Arabic and eventually making them available to European peoples. During this period, the Islamic world was far ahead of Europe with a comparatively high standard of living and intellectual accomplishment. Islamic cities had public libraries (one library in Cordoba, Spain, had 400,000 books), hospitals, universities, parks and gardens and sports stadiums. Up until very recently medical treatment in Europe was based on the work of Islamic scholars. We owe our system of Arabic numerals, the concept of zero, the compass, papermaking, algebra, and geometry to the Muslims who either invented them or improved upon them.

Muslims today look back on this period, when they were a great people, with much nostalgia, more so because of their recent history of being ruled by foreign Christian powers. The period seems very real to them, although it ended many centuries ago.

DECLINE OF ISLAM
Some time in the sixteenth century the Islamic world entered a period of decline. There is no agreement as to when this decline actually began, and as is the case with most important developments in human history, it happened gradually rather than all at once. But the results of this decline had a profound influence on Islamic thinking. For hundreds of years, Islam had been superior to Christianity in military power, standard of living, culture and learning. Then European armies began to defeat the armies of Islam regularly, European civilization caught up with and passed Islamic civilization, and soon the Islamic lands came under European occupation.

An important reason for the rise of European superiority over Islam was the growth of strong separate nation-states such as France and England in Europe. There were no separate Islamic states before the twentieth century. The European idea of a state with its own separate government, territory and laws was totally foreign to Muslims. They were members of the community of Islam, subjects of Allah, His Messenger and the "agent of the Messenger," the caliph.

The caliphate, however, had ended for all practical purposes in 1258 A.D., when its capital, Baghdad, was destroyed by nomad invaders. Gradually two centers of power developed in the Middle East, the Ottoman Turkish Empire and the Safavid Empire of Iran. For several centuries the Ottoman and Iranian armies were superior

(25)

to European armies. Then European military technology began to improve. As European countries became more and more able to defeat the armies of Islam, they began to take territories away from the Ottomans and from Iran. By the end of the nineteenth century the Ottomans had lost nearly all their Eastern European territories, and Iran had lost some of its northern provinces to Russia.

The nineteenth-century Industrial Revolution helped to establish European economic superiority over Islam. European countries, particularly France and England, set off on a mad scramble to acquire colonies in Africa, Asia and the Middle East as sources of raw materials for their new factories. The contest for colonies led them to interfere more and more frequently in the internal affairs of the Ottoman Empire and Iran.

The contest for colonies and resulting political rivalry of European powers were important factors in the outbreak of World War I in 1914. The Ottoman sultans had been able to keep the Middle East part of their empire together by playing off the European powers against each other. Because of anger with England and France— the two countries that had interfered the most, by aiding independence movements in Ottoman-controlled Greece, and by protecting Christian and Jewish minorities elsewhere in their territories—the Ottomans, in the early 1900s allied themselves with Germany. The Ottomans also admired German military efficiency.

When World War I broke out the Ottoman sultan called for a jihad against Britain and France. His call fell on deaf ears. Iran, as we will see in the next chapter, had its own troubles with European countries, and in any case the last thing on the Iranians' minds was to take up arms for the hated Ottoman sultan. Worse yet, a number of the sultan's Arab subjects were persuaded by British agents to revolt against him, with the expectation that Britian would help them establish a state of their own after the war.

(26)

World War I ended in 1918 when the Germans were defeated and the Ottomans along with them. A British general rode into Jerusalem on a white horse and a French general did the same thing in Constantinople, the Ottoman capital, symbolizing the triumph of Christianity over Islam. A peace treaty was signed and the provinces of the empire were divided up among the victorious European nations. Only a small slice of territory around the Ottoman capital was left to the sultan. For all practical purposes the sultan was a prisoner in his own house.

The division of the Ottoman provinces into territories controlled by European nations was the single most important factor in the development of Islamic conflict in the Middle East in the twentieth century. In theory the French and British were supposed to help prepare the peoples of the various provinces for self-government, each group with its own political system, national borders, national armies, constitutions and legal codes. The idea was to help them develop a sense of *nationalism*, which meant giving up the idea of an Islamic nation for the idea of separate but equal Islamic states.

Since the concept of a separate state was totally foreign to the peoples of these provinces the French and British soon found that the Syrians, Egyptians, Lebanese and other Ottoman subject peoples not only would not work with them, but also fought them as enemy occupiers.

Muslim Syrians, Muslim Iraqis, Muslim Jordanians, Muslim Egyptians and Muslim Lebanese therefore all found themselves citizens of separate states, headed by governments set up without their consent, sometimes with leaders who had been brought in from some other part of the Middle East. It is hardly surprising then that even today their sense of nationhood is not very clear, and as we will see in later chapters, they have continued to struggle with each other as if they were Muslim "brothers" rather than responsible modern nations.

(27)

4

Iran: Shah's Monarchy, Khomeini's Republic

In October 1971 Muhammad Reza Pahlavi, shah of Iran, presided over ceremonies at Persepolis, the ancient capital of the Persian Empire, marking the 2,500th anniversary of the Persian-Iranian monarchy. During this period many different dynasties came and went. But there was always a monarchy of some kind in Iran. When Muslim Arab armies occupied the country in 637 A.D. the caliph of Islam became, in effect, the king. The only difference with pre-Islamic times was that this new "king" was also the representative of Allah. Iranians are an adaptable, clever and subtle people, able to make the best of bad situations, and usually come out on top. They quickly accepted Islam and made great contributions to Islamic civilization in literature, art, architecture, medicine and the sciences. The entire pre-Islamic system of government in Iran was borrowed by the Arabs for the administration of the caliphate. This explains why after a while the caliph began to act and rule more like a Persian king than a simple agent of Allah.

We should note that although the names "Persia" and "Iran" describe the same country there is an important difference between them. The Persian Empire of

(28)

550–330 B.C. began in the province or region of Pars. The Persian language, after the Muslim Arab conquest, acquired many Arabic words and was written in the Arabic alphabet, with a few letters added. "Persia" was a name that symbolized the power of the ancient empire, while Iran, a geographical name, was adopted by the Muslim Arab conquerors. In the nineteenth century, when European powers, especially England, began to intervene in Iranian affairs they referred to the country with contempt as Persia. In 1935 Reza Shah, the new ruler who came to power after World War I and started the process of building up Iran as a modern state, changed the official name back to "Iran" to symbolize his country's new pride and strength and remind his people of their glorious past.

We said in Chapter 2 that the Shia were a minority in all Islamic countries except Iran. They became a majority in Iran in the sixteenth century. At that time an Iranian Shia tribal leader was fighting against the Ottoman Turks who were Sunni. The Ottomans were trying to add Iran to their empire. The tribal leader told the Shia religious leaders of Iran that he was a descendant of one of the Twelve Imams. In fact, he was not, but he picked an Imam about whom little was known so the religious leaders couldn't check up on him. He said that if they accepted him as ruler, he would lead a jihad against the Ottomans.

The Shia religious leaders were delighted. Not only did the agreement give them military protection but also they acquired some control over the ruler since he was, in a sense, obligated to them for his position. They called on all Iranians to accept the new ruler.

The dynasty founded by this leader, the Safavid, was the first one that was more or less dependent on the Shia religious leaders. Since then all Iranian dynasties have been required to protect Shia Islam and obey the authority of the religious leaders. Many Shia moved to

(29)

Iran to put themselves under the protection of the Iranian rulers until the Shia population became a majority. One of the main reasons for the 1978–79 revolution that overthrew the shah and established the Islamic Republic was the shah's refusal to obey Islamic law as defined by Shia religious leaders.

The establishment of the Islamic Republic has had important consequences, not only for Iran, but also for the Islamic world. In the balance of this chapter we will examine the background and circumstances that led up to the 1978–79 revolution, and the prospects for the republic. In terms of Islamic state conflict, the Iranian republic represents a high-water mark. For the first time in modern history, religious leaders have gained full control over an individual Islamic government.

The Islamic Republic of Iran set its goal from the start as a reconstruction of the original Islamic community of Muhammad. Other Islamic governments fear that the Iranian republic's example will encourage pressure on them from their own people to do away with man-made laws, nonreligious education, "Western" patterns of social freedom such as unveiled women, and other developments of the last forty years of independence. If the regime of Ayatollah Khomeini were not absorbed in internal problems, it might try to undermine leaders of these governments (as Khomeini has done, for example, with Iraqi president Saddam Hussein), or to export its revolution more actively through Shia missionaries. Whatever happens, the world of Islam will never be the same as it was before the Islamic revolution.

BACKGROUND: THE CONSTITUTIONAL REVOLUTION

In the 1800s Europe's expansion in search of colonies and sources of raw materials threatened Iran along with the other Islamic lands. The Iranian dynasty at that time, the *Qajar*, decided that Iran's only hope for survival was to modernize. This would mean developing a banking system, better roads, a telephone and telegraph service, industries and all the facilities and services that European governments provided for their citizens.

The Qajar rulers decided to give European companies or individuals concessions or leases to develop these needed services. The developer would pay fees for each concession. They would be allowed to make a profit, but each concession would have a time limit. At the end of the time limit the concession would be returned to Iran. Along with concessions, the nineteenth-century shahs allowed upper-class families who could afford it to send their sons to Europe to be educated. At that time the only schools in Iran were religious primary schools. They taught only boys. When a boy had memorized the Koran and could recite it perfectly, he was considered educated. The rulers expected that the young men educated abroad would bring back European scientific and technical knowledge that would help Iran become a modern state.

As a result of this policy Iranian students did gain some scientific knowledge. They also observed how far ahead of Iran the Europeans were in their standard of living. But the most important part of their education had to do with ideas. They studied the French Revolution with its ideas of liberty, equality, fraternity. They studied the American Revolution with its ideas of democracy, its constitution, its creed of freedom and justice for all. They returned to Iran convinced that what the country needed was a constitution and a bill of rights with limts on the absolute power of the shah.

In 1901 the shah gave a concession to an Australian geologist, William D'Arcy, to search for oil in Iran. The age of steam was just beginning, and European countries were looking for oil as the new fuel that would provide power for their fleets, dams, factories and automobiles. Soon afterward, the first Iranian oil wells went into production. A British company, Anglo-Iranian Oil Company (AIOC), was formed to run the oil industry. It got all the profits, except for a very small royalty fee paid to the Iranian government.

The oil concession made many Iranians angry, including the Constitutionalists. They saw Iran's most valuable resource being given away to foreigners. They were afraid that the next step would be occupation in which Iran would become a colony like the European colonies in Africa. The religious leaders declared that the oil concession was a threat to Islam. The bazaar merchants feared that the shah had sold out to foreign businessmen. Their own shops and businesses were being ruined by cheap imported products which supplanted things traditionally made and sold in the bazaars.

In 1906 there were riots in Teheran. The shah ruling at that time tried to put down the riots by force. The bazaar merchants closed their shops and called a general strike, and with the bazaar closed city life came to a dead stop. The shah was in a difficult position. His troops refused to shoot their own people; he could not even send for a cup of tea because the palace servants were on strike. So he gave in. He agreed to give the Iranian people a constitution. This constitution provided for an elected *Majlis* (parliament or national assembly), with the first Majlis meeting in 1907. From that time on the rulers of Iran have been required to obey the constitution.

REZA SHAH
AND THE AYATOLLAH
At the end of World War I Iran was in bad shape. British troops had occupied part of the country and, following the example of neighboring Russian provinces, a communist republic had been set up in the north. It seemed as if the country would fall apart. The authority of the shah hardly reached beyond his capital of Teheran.

At this critical time in the country's history a hero on horseback rode in from the countryside. His name was Reza Khan. He was the commander of the Cossack Brigade, a special military force organized in 1879 by Russian officers from the Cossack ethnic group, famous as warriors. Reza was over six feet tall, which was unusual for an Iranian, and in his tall beaver hat and scarlet uniform, riding a magnificent horse, he looked every inch a king, which he soon became.

Reza Khan brought order out of chaos. He overthrew the communist republic and restored the authority of the central government over all of Iran. In 1925 he was ready for kingship. The Majlis, at his request, deposed the elderly, ailing shah and proclaimed Reza Khan as Reza Shah, the first ruler of the new Pahlavi dynasty. This was a name he chose himself because it was the name of an ancient province of the Persian Empire and by using it Reza Shah thought he could encourage his people to have a sense of pride in themselves and their past.

About the time Reza Khan came riding into Teheran, a young student went to Qum to study under the great religious teachers there. He came from a family of scholars, and although he was young, he impressed his teachers with his wisdom and aptitude for learning. Soon he rose to the rank of ayatollah, the highest honor in the Shia religious hierarchy of Iran. His name was Rouhollah Mossavi Khomeini, the last name coming from Khomein, the little town where he lived.

Even then Khomeini was no stranger to violence. His father had been killed during World War I by government troops because he protested the heavy taxes imposed on the villagers. Probably this experience made the young Khomeini decide to become active in politics. Other religious leaders had gone along with the idea of a constitutional monarchy, but Khomeini believed there should be no monarchy at all because no matter what monarch was on the throne he would take advantage of his position to exploit the people.

The paths of Reza Shah and Ayatollah Khomeini crossed in the 1930s. Reza Shah's dream was to make Iran a modern nation. To reach this goal he would have to go against the religious leaders more strongly than any other monarch in Iran's history in order to break their hold over the people. He made a distinction between God's law, which was written in the Koran, and practical laws based on God's law but developed by governments for their people in the modern world. These laws should be made by legal experts, he said, and not by untrained *mullahs*, the village religious leaders. He hired European experts to write a complete code of laws for Iran.

Reza Shah did many other things that made the religious leaders angry. He ordered Iranian women to stop wearing the *chador*, a shapeless full-length black gown with a face veil which they wore when they went out in public. To emphasize the point that the chador was a symbol of the backward, ignorant condition of Iran's women, the shah's wife and daughters appeared unveiled at public programs and their pictures were published in Teheran newspapers.

Reza Shah also required all children to go to primary school, not at the village mosque but in fine new schools where they were taught "reading, writing and arithmetic." A start was made toward high-school education, and Iran's first modern university opened in 1935.

The religious leaders were angry in private, but did little to oppose the shah's ideas in public. One religious leader who criticized the shah in a sermon at the mosque was punished by having his turban pulled off and his head shaved by an army general.

The only religious leader who consistently spoke out against Reza Shah was Ayatollah Khomeini. Khomeini not only denounced the shah as an enemy of Islam, he said the shah had no right to the throne of Iran. Reza

Shah paid little attention to Khomeini, leaving the ayatollah alone in deference to his high position. The shah
knew he had the rest of the religious leaders in his pock-
et, and he believed he knew what was best for his people.
They were his children, and he was their wise, stern
father.

THE AYATOLLAH
AND THE SON

In 1941 there was violent conflict again in Iran. Nazi
Germany had invaded the Soviet Union in June of that
year, and as allies of the Soviet Union, the United States
and Britain desperately needed to get military supplies
and equipment to Soviet troops. Iran, the Soviet Union's
neighbor to the south, was the logical place for a supply
line, especially since Reza Shah had built a railroad all
the way across the country from north to south.

The British and Soviets believed that Reza Shah
might allow Iran's territory to be used for German bases
because he was known to admire German military efficiency and had hired a number of German advisers. The
British and Soviets demanded that Reza Shah get rid of
these advisers, but he appeared to be unwilling to do so,
so they invaded Iran and divided the country into two
Zones of Occupation.

Reza Shah debated what to do. His daughter, Prin-
cess Ashraf, writing many years later, remembers him
pacing back and forth in his garden. In his baggy civilian
clothes he looked old and shrunken, nothing like the tall
man on horseback who rode in triumph through Teheran
twenty-two years earlier. Reza Shah finally decided to
abdicate his throne, turning it over to his son, Crown
Prince Muhammad Reza. In that way the Pahlavi dynasty would continue. In return for his abdication, the British and the Soviets promised to respect Iran's independence and to withdraw their occupation troops after the
war.

The crown prince was twenty-two years old, and had

(35)

been under his father's powerful thumb all his life. As he rode through the streets of Teheran to take the formal constitutional oath of office before the Majlis in 1941, it seemed unlikely that he would rule his country for thirty-seven years, and even less likely that he would leave Iran as the last "King of Kings" in 2,500 years of monarchy. And in fact, for many years of his reign, Shah Muhammad Reza was neither a strong nor a popular leader. Senior advisers from his father's generation told him what to do. His father had never been popular with the people, and it seemed unlikely that his own shy, self-absorbed personality would change enough for him to become a strong leader.

One morning in 1949, however, as the shah was leaving Teheran University after making a speech, a man wearing a press photographer's badge stepped forward and fired six pistol shots at him from point-blank range, six feet away. Not one of the bullets found its mark. The shah decided then and there that Allah had saved him in order for him to continue his father's work of making Iran into a modern nation. He was convinced that he would neither die nor be defeated until the job was done.

In spite of his new belief in his mission for Iran, it took many years for the shah to feel secure about his power. He nearly lost his throne in 1953 when the prime minister, Muhammad Mossadegh, led a move to nationalize the Iranian oil industry. The move came about because the Anglo-Iranian Oil Company refused to accept a new contract with the Iranian government which would give Iran a fifty-fifty split in oil royalties. The shah opposed the nationalization, saying that Iran was not ready to run its own oil industry. But Mossadegh continued his opposition in spite of the shah.

Conflict between the shah and Mossadegh, who was supported by the communist Tudeh Party, came to a head in 1953. The oil industry had almost shut down because the United States and other industrial nations were boycotting Iran, and times were hard for most of the Iranian people. Mossadegh and the Tudeh blamed the shah for the country's troubles and he blamed them. The United States feared a communist takeover through the Tudeh, while Mossadegh was saying openly that the shah should be deposed as a traitor to Islam and the tool of foreign powers.

The United States organized a counter-plot against Mossadegh and the Tudeh, emphasizing the communist danger to Iran. The army remained loyal to the shah, and while the monarch rested in Rome, Italy, on a brief "vacation," army generals crushed the opposition. Mossadegh was arrested and the Tudeh Party broken up, as most Iranians decided they preferred royalty to communism. They were more positive of their allegiance when oil production resumed under a new contract which gave Iran 50 percent of the royalties from oil exports.

The events of 1953 convinced the shah that he was destined to lead Iran to greatness as a strong leader. However, growing numbers of Iranians felt that he owed his throne to American help. The feeling of Iran being again dependent upon foreign powers, the United States in particular, increased steadily in the 1960s to a peak in the 1970s. Also, although Mossadegh was under house arrest (he died in 1966) he was considered by many Iranians to have acted as a sincere patriot. The feeling of subservience to foreign powers and the conviction that the shah had unfairly judged Mossadegh were to be underlying factors in the 1978–79 revolution.

Revolution, however, was a long way from peoples' thoughts in the 1950s. The shah thought mainly about building up his power and about his program of greatness for Iran. To insure his position he began developing a strong army, equipped with the latest weapons purchased from the United States. He outlawed the Tudeh Party, and broke up the National Front, a loose political organ-

(37)

ization that had grown up around Mossadegh. The shah decreed that Iran would have no political parties as they were sources of conflict and instability and would never work for the good of the country.

In 1963 the shah was ready for the second phase of Iran's "March to Greatness," when he announced his own "revolution." He called it the "Shah-to-People" Program, but it is usually referred to as the "White Revolution." One Iranian writer said at the time that it should be called the White Revolution because it was prepared in the White House!

The White Revolution included such reforms as land distribution, literacy programs and the right of women to vote. The reforms sounded good but the religious leaders criticized them. They said that the lands being distributed were mostly those confiscated by Reza Shah in the first place without compensation to the owners. The problem, as the religious leaders saw it, was that, although the shah might have had good intentions, his foundation which distributed the land did not give clear title to the new peasant owners, nor any means of financing the development of the land. They further objected to giving women the right to vote because they thought this reform would undermine Islam. They said the White Revolution would bring more foreigners into Iran and make the country even more dependent upon foreign powers than it already was.

From his home in Qum, Ayatollah Khomeini made a number of angry speeches denouncing the White Revolution. Other religious leaders spoke out in other cities, and called upon their followers to protest. There were riots throughout the country. But the shah of those days was still the stern father. Army and police forces put down the riots with heavy casualties, and Khomeini was arrested. The shah, however, did not want to give the opposition a martyr by killing the ayatollah or putting him in jail. The shah decided instead to send Khomeini

(38)

out of the country permanently. He was exiled to Turkey first, and then because the Turks did not want him, to Iraq. The Sunni leaders of Iraq said he could stay as long as he did not criticize their government or their policies toward Iraq's large Shia minority. They did not care, though, what he said about the shah and this was to be an important factor in the revolution of 1978–79.

KHOMEINI'S REVOLUTION

Wendell Phillips, American antislavery writer in the nineteenth century, once wrote: "Revolutions are not made. They come. A revolution is as natural a growth as an oak. Its foundations are laid back in history." The 1978–79 revolution in Iran proves his point. It completed the constitutional revolution of 1906, as the Iranians believed the Pahlavi shahs had ruled without regard for the constitution or proper respect for Islam. The revolution set aside the "White Revolution," which had seemed to bring more problems than benefits to the people. Because Ayatollah Khomeini had led the protests against the White Revolution and had been exiled for his opposition, his exile made him a martyr after all to the revolutionary cause. There was no doubt in people's minds after 1963 that Khomeini was the leader of the anti-shah movement, and in 1978 many Iranians began to call him Imam Khomeini as if the twelfth Imam had returned.

Fifteen or sixteen years is not a long time in terms of Iran's 2,500 years of monarchy, yet to the Iranian revolutionaries it must have seemed not only a long time, but, at times, a hopeless struggle. Their task was made more difficult by the economic boom, particularly after 1973 when oil prices tripled. Billions of dollars now poured into the country. A great deal of the money was spent on military equipment, and there was much mismanagement, corruption and high inflation. Some Iranians— perhaps 20 percent of the population—benefited directly from the boom, but the majority of the people—peasants, small shopkeepers and blue-collar workers—did not benefit. The sudden wealth was disturbing to the religious leaders who felt that the basic fabric of Islam was being further weakened.

Organized opposition to the shah gathered momentum in the late 1970s. Although Ayatollah Khomeini was in exile, he was not far away. Khomeini continued to denounce the shah in speech after speech, and tapes of his speeches were smuggled into Iran and read aloud as sermons by the mullahs in the mosques.

The open conflict that ended with the fall of the shah began with a demonstration at Qum in 1978, put down by the police with great brutality. Two mullahs were killed and their bloody turbans draped over the entry to the main mosque. Demonstrations followed in city after city with tape recordings made on the spot to show the brutality and oppressiveness of the regime.

As the cycle of violence continued the shah seemed to lose control of the situation. The advisers he had depended on for many years had grown old and many had died. His new advisers did not have enough experience or wisdom to tell him what to do. He could no longer bring himself to use the power he had, for that would mean killing many thousands of his own people. At the same time he could not bring himself to compromise with his old enemy Khomeini.

As it turned out, the shah had no chance for compromise. On September 8, 1978—a day that became known in the revolution as Black Friday—the massacre of several thousand demonstrators by the shah's troops in Teheran forced his hand. In response to strikes called throughout the country to protest the massacre, the shah cancelled twenty-billion-dollars in orders for U.S. aircraft, ordered wage increases for the strikers, and announced amnesties for several thousand political prisoners. But it was too little, too late.

The key to the success of the revolution was the sudden departure of Khomeini from Iraq for Paris, France. Iraq had yielded to pressure from the shah to expel Khomeini in October 1978. The shah thought that sending Khomeini out of Iraq would remove him from contact with his fellow religious leaders and supporters in Iran. But when Khomeini got to Paris he was able to go directly to his people by telephone (there is no direct Iraq-Iran telephone service). And from his new residence he was able to bring the cause of the Iranian people before world public opinion. The eyes of the world, and the world press, were focused on a Shia graybeard in a black turban who called himself the "Shadow of Allah" and said he was carrying on a jihad on behalf of the twelfth Imam. It was a statement that millions of Iranians believed as they went out into the streets to fight for the ayatollah. Faced with the total opposition of his people, the shah abdicated and left the country with his family in January 1979.

THE ISLAMIC REPUBLIC
OF IRAN

On February 1, 1979, Ayatollah Rouhollah Khomeini returned to a hero's welcome in his native land after almost sixteen years of exile. He declared that Iran would be henceforth an Islamic Republic, headed by a Revolutionary Council of religious leaders with himself as the supreme leader and interpreter of Islamic law. Later in the year a new constitution was drafted, placing final authority over the nation in the hands of a supreme leader chosen from among the religious leaders. The Revolutionary Council was replaced by a Council of Guardians—religious leaders—headed by Khomeini; it was supposedly above politics, and indeed one of the republic's few assets in its early stages was Khomeini's ability to stay above political infighting and reconcile opposing views.

(41)

An American columnist observed recently that Iran seemed to most Americans to be like the land of Oz, everything there being strange and a bit out of whack. An air of unreality, like a curtain of smog, still hangs over the republic after three years of survival. Continued violence, economic problems caused by reduced oil production, a war with Sunni Iraq, internal conflicts with Sunni minorities (Kurdish and Arab) and much internal violence have caused great difficulties for the republic.

The revolution was costly to the republic in a number of ways. Reaction to the brutality of the shah's regime led to counter-brutality as Iranians who had been mistreated, tortured or jailed rushed to settle old scores. The religious leader in charge of state trials, Ayatollah Khalkhali, boasted of personal responsibility for two hundred executions. The great majority of Iran's skilled professionals left the country. Many of them had supported the revolution, but there seemed to be no place for them in Khomeini's "Government of Allah," ruled by fundamentalist religious leaders.

Along with the departure of skilled professionals there developed a shortage of leadership. Since the shah had never allowed honest criticism of his policies or dissent, people associated with his regime were automatically considered yes-men and were not to be trusted.

What are the prospects for the Islamic Republic of Iran? In assessing its future we need to think in Iranian terms—see their country as they do. One major difference between Iranians and Americans is that the Iranian outlook on life is fundamentally religious: Shia Islam touches all aspects of Iranian life.

The problem for Iranians, and for that matter all Muslims, is how to reconcile twentieth-century life with the requirements of their religion. We mentioned the exodus of most of Iran's skilled managerial-technical people. No doubt in time others will replace them, but for now Khomeini has said that Iran does not need all

(42)

that oil wealth or Western technology and would, in fact, be better off without them.

The Islamic Republic is also unusual in that religious leaders are directly involved in the day-to-day management of the government. Their involvement comes partly by default as no other leadership is available. It also stems from the strong religious organization of Shia Islam. But direct control of a government by religious leaders historically has its limits, especially when these leaders are untrained in national affairs.

In 1980 the Iranian religious leaders declared a cultural revolution, which is still going on, to purge the country of all non-Islamic influences. This revolution within a revolution aroused violent conflict between the religious leaders and various groups such as the Marxist Fedayeen who advocate an Islamic republic that is socialist in nature.

Because of the Iranian people's sense of their long history as a nation, no matter what conflicts they become involved in, whether internal or external, they will endure. Their sense of their superiority as a people and their invincibility against foreign imposition of ideals as well as material and technological advances will prove to be both a strength and a weakness as they attempt to cope with living in the twentieth century with their faces turned resolutely back to the six hundreds A.D.

(43)

5

The Arabs, One Nation Divided

We noted in Chapter 3 that France and England began to interfere in the internal affairs of the Ottoman Empire in the nineteenth century. The French and the British were most concerned with the condition of the Christian population in the Arab provinces of the Empire, corresponding to modern Syria, Lebanon, Jordan and Palestine (Israel). Along with the Jews, Greeks, Armenians and various Christian sects living in these provinces, there were a large number of Christian Arabs. They were Arab in language and culture, and thought of themselves as Arabs in contrast to the non-Arab Ottomans who ruled them. But their religion was denominational Christianity. As the French, British, and later American missionaries established schools and colleges for the sultan's Christian subjects in the Arab provinces, a number of Christian Arab children attended along with their Greek, Armenian and other Christian compatriots.

ARAB NATIONALISM: THE BEGINNINGS
Arab nationalism, the movement to establish a separate Arab nation, first as a self-governing part of the Otto-

(44)

man Empire, and then, after World War I, as a single independent state, really began in these European colleges. As more and more Christian Arabs attended them, they became concerned about the low position of the Arabs in the Ottoman Empire. The Arabs in the empire were treated as second- or even third-class subjects, although theoretically all subjects of the sultan were equal. The Arabs had no officials of their own, as did other groups, but were ruled by Ottoman officials. No one represented the Arabs before the law and they were discriminated against in countless other ways.

In 1875 students at the American mission-founded Syrian Protestant College in Beirut, Lebanon (now the American University of Beirut), formed a secret club called the Syrian Scientific Society. The members, encouraged by the classes they took with American teachers and the ideas they learned about freedom, democracy and human rights, talked of an Arab nation free of Ottoman control. Their Arab nation would include all Arabs in the Ottoman provinces. It would still be a part of the Islamic world, but would have its own Arab leaders, use Arabic instead of Turkish as its official language and reawaken Arabs everywhere to a sense of their own greatness. It would bring Christian and Muslim Arabs together in a harmonious unit, living the way Christian, Muslim and Jew had lived in Islamic Spain centuries ago.

This was the beginning of the Arab national movement, also called "Arab nationalism" and sometimes Pan Arabism. As we have said, it was not in the beginning an Islamic nationalism.

Around the year 1900 conflict began to develop between Arabs and Turks. The sultan still ruled, but the power of his empire had faded. At the beginning of the twentieth century, however, a group of young officers and government officials called the Young Turks wanted to revive the Ottoman Empire, to make it the equal of the

European powers, at least militarily. They were sure they could not count on the Arabs for any help; after all, a leading Muslim Arab writer in Cairo, Egypt, had published a book listing twenty-six reasons why the Arabs were better Muslims than the Turks, and should therefore have the office of caliph back.

The Ottomans cracked down on Arab societies and groups they suspected of working for the cause of an "Arab nation" independent of the sultan. Arab leaders were arrested or sent to the Ottoman capital, Constantinople, where the sultan could keep an eye on them.

WORLD WAR I—
THE ARAB REVOLT

When World War I broke out the Arabs thought they had a good chance to establish their nation. The British army in Egypt was planning campaigns against the Arab provinces of the Ottoman Empire, as part of its strategy for defeating the Ottomans, Germany's ally. British agents in Egypt began to make secret contacts with Arab leaders, urging them to revolt against the sultan.

The British did not have a very high opinion of the Arabs. Their most famous secret agent, T. E. Lawrence, wrote in his book *Seven Pillars of Wisdom* that "Arabs could be swung on an idea as on a cord, for the unpledged allegiance of their minds made them obedient servants." In encouraging the Arabs to revolt, the British made certain promises to the Arab leaders that were to be the cause of much bitterness and conflict in later years.

The most prominent Arab leader at the time of the war was the Grand Sherif Hussein of Mecca, the great-grandfather of King Hussein of Jordan. "Grand Sherif" was the title he held in his position as guardian of the holy cities of Islam and the official in charge of the annual pilgrimage. The British approached Sherif Hussein and asked if he would be willing to call a *jihad* on behalf of the Arabs against the sultan. In return the British promised to help the Arabs establish a nation of their own once the Ottomans had been defeated.

The Grand Sherif of Mecca believed the British promise He wrote a letter to Sir Henry MacMahon, the top British official in Egypt, in which he laid out Arab conditions for a revolt against the Ottomans. His main conditions were that Britain and its French allies would recognize an independent Arab nation consisting of the Arab provinces of the Ottoman Empire, and that the British would help this new Arab nation get on its feet after the war had ended.

Sir Henry MacMahon's reply to Sherif Hussein was evasive. He said that his government accepted the general principle of Arab independence and the right of the Arabs to have their own nation in areas where they were a majority of the population. Britain was also prepared to make Hussein king of this new Arab nation. But that was as far as the British would go.

Sherif Hussein decided that the British were men of their word. He called his sons together and told them to organize a revolt against the Ottomans. His two younger sons, Abdullah and Faisal, were given the job of getting an army together. It would be made up mostly of bedouin horsemen, the same men whose ancestors rode out of the desert to conquer a large part of the world for Islam thirteen centuries earlier.

The story of the Arab Revolt of 1916–17 is an exciting story. Arab raiders, led by Faisal and T. E. Lawrence, struck suddenly at Ottoman supply lines, blew up warehouses and oil-storage tanks, and then disappeared. The Hejaz Railroad, the main line from northern Arab cities south to Mecca, was put out of commission. Ottoman garrisons were shut up in ports and the towns along the rail line. In 1917 a British army joined the Arabs to drive the Ottomans out of the Arab provinces.

(47)

THE ARABS DIVIDED:
THE MANDATE SYSTEM

It seemed then that a centuries-old dream was about to come true for the Arabs. But then history turned wrong, resulting in a sort of psychological sickness which fell like a plague upon them. The Arabs discovered that the British had not only made promises to them, but had at the same time made certain secret agreements with their French and Russian allies to divide up the entire Ottoman Empire into colonies.

At first Sherif Hussein could not believe that the British had misled him. He was confident that they would keep their promise, and he began preparations for the great day just ahead for the Arab nation. He named Ali, his oldest son, as Amir (Prince) of the Hejaz. Then his second son, Faisal, led the Arab army to Damascus and was hailed by thousands of Syrian Arabs as king of Syria. Hussein himself was content to wait for the abdication of the defeated Ottoman sultan. When that happened, he would declare himself the caliph of all Islam.

But the British and the French had other plans. French troops occupied Lebanon and then Syria. Faisal's Arab horsemen were no match for French artillery and tanks, and Faisal wound up back at his father's house in Mecca. British troops occupied Palestine. The British government said that because Palestine was sacred to three religions—Christianity, Judaism, and Islam—it could not possibly belong only to the Arabs. The British also controlled Iraq and the region "beyond the river Jordan" which was marked vaguely on maps as Transjordan.

Under the terms of the peace treaty between the French and British and the defeated Ottoman Empire, the newly formed League of Nations assigned the Arab provinces of the empire to Britain and France as mandates. Each province would be under French or British control for vaguely stated time periods determined by the controlling power. At the end of that period it was assumed that the province would be ready for independence. Syria and Lebanon went to France; Iraq, Transjordan and Palestine, to Britain. Subsequently the French divided Syria and Lebanon into two mandates.

To sweeten the bitter pill of broken promises to Sherif Hussein and to satisfy the League of Nations, the British chose two of his sons to head the governments of their mandates. They brought Faisal back from Mecca as the first king of Iraq. The area called Transjordan was organized into a mandate headed by Amir (Prince) Abdullah, with a new capital, Amman, rising out of the dusty hills and ruins of the ancient Roman city of Philadelphia. There was no place in the British scheme of things for the Sherif's eldest son, Ali, and in the 1920s another friend of Britain, an Arab tribal chief named Ibn Saud, chased Ali and his father from Mecca and established what is today the Kingdom of Saudi Arabia.

THE COLONIAL LEGACY

The legacy of the European powers to the Arabs was a group of sovereign states, each with its own government, laws, national identity (Syrian, Lebanese and so on) and definite borders. According to the theory that half a loaf is better than none, the Arabs might have been satisfied to wind up with two kings plus a schedule for independence that might allow them to unite eventually into a single Arab nation. But instead of a steady progress toward unity, the legacy to the Arabs has been one of conflict, disagreement and occasionally war.

The French and British drafted constitutions for the mandates. The French set up Syria and Lebanon as French-style republics with French laws, French schools and universities, and an elected president and legislature. But real power was in the hands of the French high commissioner, backed by the French army and police.

(49)

The British were somewhat less strict in their mandates, in part because they had two popular Arab leaders (Faisal and Abdullah). A British high commissioner was appointed to head the government under each ruler. Because Transjordan was mostly tribal desert country, the British were able to find a loyal group of tribal chiefs to work with King Abdullah.

Iraq had a mixed population with a large number of Shia Arabs, a slightly larger number of Arab Sunnis, plus Sunni Kurds, Christians and Jews, bedouin tribes and a number of other groups left over from Babylonian times. The British trusted only a small group of tribal chiefs, wealthy landowners and former officers in the Ottoman army.

Some positive results of the colonial legacy should be mentioned. All four mandates benefited economically, with schools, hospitals and modern buildings built by the Europeans to make up for centuries of Ottoman neglect. European officers trained their Syrian, Iraqi, Transjordanian and Lebanese counterparts in preparation for independence when they would supposedly have their own national armies. The new schools brought to a new generation of young Arabs a sense of national identity as Syrians, Lebanese, Iraqis and Jordanians which was weak at the beginning but which eventually became nearly as strong as the drive for Arab unity.

INTERNAL CONFLICT IN IRAQ
Iraq was the first mandate to gain its independence, in 1932. The British sponsored Iraq as a member of the League of Nations and it was the first Arab country to be admitted. But Iraq was not yet a nation; it was a collection of mutually hostile groups ruled by a Sunni Arab king. Most Iraqis still considered Faisal to be a tool of Britain, incapable of acting on his own or Iraq's best interests. Many Iraqis also felt that their country was not completely independent. They pointed to the British air

(50)

bases which were off-limits to Iraqis without special permission because the latest British planes and equipment were kept there. The British-owned Iraq Petroleum Company (IPC) controlled Iraqi oil production. As was the case with Iran, Iraq got about thirty cents on the dollar in royalties per barrel of oil.

Many Iraqis also saw the British as interfering in their government to make sure that national leaders unfriendly to Britain would not become too powerful. The British favorite among Iraqi leaders was Colonel (later General) Nuri al-Said, who was prime minister many times during the monarchy (1932–1958).

General Nuri, as he was usually called, was not much of a military man, but a clever politician. He was able to gain the confidence of the British, work with the king, and play off his rivals in the constant power struggle around the throne. Nuri once said cynically of the Iraqi leadership that it reminded him of a small pack of cards: "You must shuffle them often, because the same faces keep turning up."

The old pack of cards included very few Shia, Kurdish, Christian or other minority faces. It also had no faces from the growing middle class of educated professional people or the British-trained officer corps, all of whom benefited from economic and educational opportunities under the mandate. The little circle around King Faisal and his successors paid little attention to this middle class, and even less to the peasants, who with no hope of improving their lives, found an outlet for their anger and frustration in conflict and violence—even in murder.

Faisal died in 1933, and was succeeded by his son Gazi, who was killed in a car accident in 1939. Gazi's uncle, Prince Abd al-Ilah, then ruled as regent for Gazi's young son Faisal II until the latter reached the age of twenty-one in 1953.

Iraq has suffered since independence from both

internal and external conflict which has been violent, unpredictable and usually unexpected. The first military coup in the Arab world was carried out by a group of Iraqi generals in 1936. In 1941 four army colonels marched troops to Baghdad, chased the regent and the young king into exile and installed an anti-British government. The result of this coup was the "Thirty-Days War" between Britain and Iraq. It ended in the defeat of the Iraqis, as British troops poured into the country from other parts of the Middle East. Once again it seemed to the majority of the Iraqis that Britain had interfered with them and taken away their right to independence as an Arab state.

There were periodic uprisings and conflicts during the next seventeen years, most of them by peasants or tribal groups protesting cruel treatment by landlords or greedy government officials. But those at the top paid little attention. Iraq seemed to outsiders to be a reasonably stable country. In 1955, along with Turkey, Iran, Pakistan and Britain, it became a member of the newly formed Baghdad Pact, a regional pact organized by Britain and the United States to block Soviet expansion into the Middle East. General Nuri, either from behind the scenes or out in front, continued to shuffle the cards and pull the strings.

The Iraqi monarchy came to an abrupt end on July 14, 1958. Army units led by the lower-ranking officers scorned by General Nuri and his associates, seized Baghdad in a lightning coup. The king, the regent, other members of the royal family, Nuri al-Said and other government leaders were executed. Iraq became an Arab republic.

Iraq's new leader, an army brigadier (equivalent to colonel), was Abd al-Karim Qassim. He was even less successful than his predecessors in dealing with the causes of conflict in the country, as communists now came out into the open, Kurds mounted open rebellion beginning in 1961, and other groups fought for a share of power. Qassim lasted five years. Then he was overthrown by his chief associate, executed gangland style in his office, and the remains of his mangled body were shown on national television. A bloody massacre of Qassim's supporters, communists and others followed.

As was the case with the massacre of the royal family in 1958, the slaughter of Qassim and his supporters underlines the element of violence in Iraqi life. Arabs generally are a volatile, violence-prone people, but Iraqis more so than other groups, in part because of the sharp economic differences between classes and the frustration of the lower classes with their miserable circumstances. The breakdown of the old stable chief-tribe, landlord-peasant relationship of prerepublic days has also increased Iraqi instability.

After a period of more-or-less stable rule, Qassim's successors were overthrown in 1968 by a group of military officers and civilians belonging to the Baath (Ba'th) Party. Since this party began in Syria, its history and involvement with inter-Arab conflict will be dealt with in the next chapter. The Iraqi Baath Party, originally a branch of the Syrian Baath, has been in power since 1968, ruling with an iron hand, although officially Iraq is an Arab republic, with a legislature, a civilian government and protection for the rights of the Shia and other minority groups. Underscoring its Arabness, the government refers to the country in official correspondence as "The Iraqi region of the Arab Homeland."

EXTERNAL CONFLICT:
THE WAR WITH IRAN
Earlier in this chapter we said that the Arabs did not have a clear idea of the borders of their Arab nation which would include all the territories where Arabs lived. The European powers, however, were quick to solve that problem. Iraq's borders were fixed by the British who

called the country Mesopotamia until 1932, when it became the Arab Kingdom of Iraq. There was a dispute between the new Republic of Turkey and Britain in the 1920s about the northern region of Iraq around the city of Mosul, which was populated mostly by Kurds. The League of Nations, on Britain's request, gave the region to Iraq. The British also, because they were more powerful than Iran, established the Iran-Iraq border along the Iranian side of the Shatt al-Arab (the delta formed by the Tigris and Euphrates rivers) instead of in the middle of the channel as the Iranians claimed it should be, under the law of international waterways. As the Iranians grew stronger they claimed ownership out to mid-channel, and sent gunboats periodically to blockade Iraqi oil tankers or barges on the Iranian side of the waterway. They also forced them to take on Iranian pilots or fly the Iranian flag. The Iraqis protested, and as a result there were artillery duels and gun battles between Iranian and Iraqi patrol boats from time to time.

The dispute became serious in the 1970s when the shah began to help the Iraqi Kurds who had been battling the government for a long time for self-government in their northern mountain region. The shah gave the Kurds military equipment and allowed Kurdish guerrillas to cross safely into Iranian territory where the Iraqi army could not follow them.

In March 1975 the shah suddenly reached an agreement with Iraqi vice-president (later President) Saddam Hussein, over border differences. The shah's ambition was for Iran to become the dominant power in the region of the Persian Gulf ("Arab Gulf" to the Arabs). A deal with Iraq would help him achieve this goal. Iraq agreed to recognize Iran's control over the Shatt al-Arab up to mid-channel. In return, the shah called off his support for the Kurds and their revolt promptly collapsed.

Many Iraqi leaders and a large part of the population felt that Saddam Hussein had bartered away Iraqi territory. They wanted a chance to strike back. This

(54)

chance came in 1980. It seemed to be also a chance for Saddam Hussein to strengthen his new position as president and earn popularity for the Baath Party by appealing to Iraqi Arab national feelings. He had just succeeded President Hassan al-Bakr, who retired because of ill health. Iraqi forces, in September 1980, invaded Iran's Khuzistan Province along the border northeast of the Shatt al-Arab. Saddam Hussein denounced the 1975 agreement as "null and void," and again claimed the entire Shatt al-Arab, from bank to bank, as Iraqi territory.

The Iraqis certainly expected a quick victory in the war. They captured the Iranian port of Khorramshahr, besieged several other Iranian cities near the border, and left Iran's major oil refinery on Abadan Island a heap of ruins. But early Iraqi expectations of a quick victory were dashed by the strong resistance of the Iranian army and air force. The war became even more a national cause for Iranians than it had been for the Iraqis. The Arabs of Khuzestan did not rise in rebellion to support their Sunni Iraqi "cousins," as the prospect of being ruled by a distant government in Baghdad was even less appealing than their expectations for self-government under Ayatollah Khomeini's "Islamic Republic."

The Iraqis also showed up badly in land and air battles. Their military equipment, most of it supplied by the Soviet Union, was not as new or as effective as the Iranian equipment, previously bought from America by the shah. The Iraqis were unable to follow up their early successes, and the war settled down to a stalemate. Unfortunately for Iraq, the longer the war went on the less support for it there was among the population. Iraqis found that the "good life" they had begun to lead as a result of the money pouring into the country from high oil prices was not as good as it had been. Food was in short supply, goods piled up in blockaded Iraqi ports and the oil industry was damaged by Iranian air attacks.

The war split the Islamic states into opposing

camps, with unexpected results. Jordan and Saudi Arabia supported Iraq, although their monarchies had often been targets of Iraqi Baathist criticism. They feared Khomeini's Shia fundamentalism with its revolutionary example might encourage their own Shia minorities to revolt if they were successful in their war against Iraq. Syria, however, backed Iran because of the rivalry between the Syrian and Iraqi Baath parties.

The Iraq-Iran war remained a stalemate until the spring of 1982 when the rebuilt Iranian army launched a series of offensives against Iraqi positions. The attacks drove Iraqi troops back inside their own border on the Shatt al-Arab. In May the Iranians recaptured the port of Khorramshahr. Previously Iran had insisted on Iraqi withdrawal from its territory and payment of about fifty billion dollars in war damages. But with its new successes, Iran's demands became more stringent. An Iranian government official said: "We have lost thousands of lives and many of our cities have been destroyed. . . . It is our right to ask for the overthrow of the Saddam Hussein regime by the Iraqi people."

That either government could topple the other as a result of the war seemed unlikely since no territorial demands except for control over the Shatt al-Arab, important for oil shipments, were involved. One positive step insofar as Iraq was concerned was the organization by Saddam Hussein of a "National Progressive Front," including representatives of other groups beside the Baath Party, as an advisory body to the government. Previously the Baath had fiercely resisted all efforts to share its power with other groups.

IMPLICATIONS OF THE WAR
The possibility of a complete military defeat for Iraq raised the specter of a replacement of Saddam Hussein by another Baath leader, although the lack of organized political opposition to the party made it unlikely that the

Baath government itself would be overthrown. Iraq's military equipment lost in the war was mostly replaced; even so, Iraq no longer had the strong military position and consequent political leverage in regional affairs it had had at the start of the war.

Even without total victory and Hussein's overthrow, Iran stood to gain significantly from the war. The Iranians saw it as a Shia jihad against Sunnis, uniting them in a holy struggle against the foreign invader. Khomeini's personal feud with Saddam Hussein, brought about by the ayatollah's expulsion from Iraq in 1978, intensified Iranian feelings; they saw the action as aimed against the agent of the twelfth Imam, their revered spiritual leader.

Several other Middle East Islamic states—in particular Turkey, Jordan and Saudi Arabia—stated their support for Iraq but refrained from committing forces or calling for volunteers to go to the front. Saudi Arabia attempted on several occasions, without success, to mediate a peace settlement. The conflict, however, between the two strongest Islamic states in the Persian Gulf, with the consequent weakening of their military power, meant that Saudi Arabia itself might in the end replace Iran and Iraq as "policeman of the Gulf."

THE HASHIMITE KINGDOM OF JORDAN

As we said earlier in this chapter, Jordan—or Transjordan—was assigned to the British as a mandate after World War I, under the leadership of Prince Abdullah. Although it was a mandate, it was actually governed as a colony by the British. Before World War I the population of this area beyond the Jordan River was made up chiefly of bedouin tribes, as the region is a continuation of the Arabian desert. Transjordan had never been a state or even an Ottoman province, but Abdullah was quite acceptable to Transjordan's people as a ruler. His ancestor, Hashim, was the founder of the clan in Mecca to which Muhammad the Messenger of God belonged. Abdullah met the requirements for the ideal Islamic Arab ruler—he was related to Muhammad, his family, the Hashimites, had a long tradition of able leadership, and he had distinguished himself in the Arab Revolt during World War I. Britain provided an annual subsidy and a team of British officers headed by General John Bagot Glubb to train a small elite Transjordanian army called the Arab Legion.

Transjordan was not affected by either external or internal conflict until shortly after World War II. Then the end of the British mandate over Palestine, which included the West Bank of the Jordan River, as opposed to the Transjordanian East Bank, brought about, in 1948, a violent conflict between Jews and Arabs. Transjordan found itself in the thick of the war. The Arab Legion marched into Palestine and occupied the West Bank and the Old City of Jerusalem, with its shrines sacred to Judaism, Christianity and Islam. West Bank leaders said they would accept Abdullah as ruler of both banks of the Jordan River. In 1950 Transjordan became the Hashimite Kingdom of Jordan under King Abdullah.

Jordan's change of status brought the country into the middle of Middle Eastern conflict for two reasons: first, its location next door to the newly created state of Israel; and second, the presence within its new borders of a large Muslim Palestinian population. The Palestinians had been under direct British control for the period of the mandate. They were better educated, lived better, and were nearly all city or small-town people. They looked down their noses at the tribal people and villagers of Transjordan. The Palestinians bitterly resented King Abdullah for having taken over the West Bank instead of helping them defeat the Israelis. In 1951 a Palestinian member of a group called *Jihad Muqaddas* ("Holy

(58)

Struggle") assassinated Abdullah outside a mosque in Jerusalem. Abdullah was succeeded by his eldest son, Talal, who was under treatment for a mental illness and was deposed by his advisers in 1953 in favor of *his* eldest son, Hussein I, now in his twenty-ninth year of rule.

Since 1967, when the Jordanian army was defeated by the Israelis and lost the West Bank territory and the Old City of Jerusalem to Israel, Hussein's kingdom has not been involved in direct conflict with any of its neighbors. Jordan did not take part in the 1973 Arab-Israeli war and, as of this writing, has taken no position on the 1982 Israeli invasion of Lebanon.

This would be consistent with King Hussein's policy of moderation in all statements about other Arab leaders, many of whom hate him and would be happy to see him overthrown despite his long-established commitment to Arab unity and his position as head of a front-line state·in the struggle with Israel.

Why do some Arab leaders hate Hussein? One reason may be envy of the diminutive king's survival record. His is the longest-running rule of any head of state presently in power in the Middle East, having outlasted Presidents Nasser and Sadat in Egypt, the shah of Iran, several Syrian and Iraqi presidents, three Saudi Arabian kings and a number of Lebanese politicians. Another reason may be his ability to keep U.S. support while simultaneously receiving large amounts of money from oil-rich Arab states as a defender of the Arab cause against Israel.

But the most important reason for Arab hostility toward Hussein is his relationship with the Palestinians. Although this book is concerned with Islamic-state conflict, the Palestinian people and their cause are a thread running through all Arab-state relations, and King Hussein's relationship with them is crucial. Therefore, a brief description of the Palestine National Movement is in order.

The Palestinians—the non-Jewish, mostly Muslim population of the Ottoman province and British mandate of Palestine—left their homeland in large numbers after the state of Israel was declared in 1948 at the end of the British mandate, and when the Israelis defeated invading Arab armies. The great majority of these refugees settled in Jordan, though about 170,000 went to Lebanon and others went to Egypt and Syria. For the most part they settled in refugee camps, but a minority, educated and intelligent, were able to move out of the camps, often to other Arab countries, and establish themselves in various professions or governments. Those who stayed in the camps were a broken, defeated people, living on United Nations assistance.

Jordan was the only Arab country to give citizenship to the Palestinians, and up until 1964 the policy of other Arab countries was to accept them where necessary but not to take any action on their behalf that might provoke an Israeli reaction. You could say that the Palestinians were an embarrassment to Arab leaders, a reminder of their military ineptness against Israel.

In 1964 the Arab leaders changed their minds, deciding that the Palestinians would be useful against Israel. They sponsored the development of the Palestine Liberation Organization (PLO), first led by a Palestinian lawyer and after 1967 by Yassir Arafat, a graduate of American University in Beirut who had been working in Kuwait. Arafat had previously (1965) founded al-Fatah (an Arabic acronym for "Movement for the Liberation of the Palestinian Homeland"). Al-Fatah became the dominant group in the PLO, but other groups scattered as far away as Damascus, Syria, were part of the organization. Although they now supported a Palestinian state, most Arab countries kept a tight rein on the PLO and refused to allow Palestinian raids from their territories into Israel. Jordan and Lebanon were the two exceptions.

(60)

In 1968 a group of al-Fatah guerrillas, with the help of the Jordanian army, inflicted heavy casualties on the Israelis at the town of Karameh, a PLO base on the occupied West Bank. Jordan's apparent support was a signal to the Palestinians, and the PLO began to build up its forces in Jordan until its strength nearly equaled that of the Jordanian army. The Palestinians seemed to be running the country. They collected money from Jordanians by force, carried their weapons in public (despite a law prohibiting it), and even took over directing traffic in Amman, Jordan's capital.

In September 1970 Hussein decided that the Palestinian threat to his regime was more serious than the possibility that Israel would attack Jordan because of the PLO. Jordanian army units pinned down the Palestinians in their camps and urban bases, while tanks rumbled through the streets of Amman. Nearly four thousand Palestinian guerrillas were killed; the remainder fled into Syria or Lebanon. The month was named "Black September" by the Palestinians. They have yet to reach the powerful position they held in Hussein's kingdom at that time, and their defeat helped insure a long reign for the courageous Hashimite monarch.

THE ARABIAN PENINSULA

The Arabian Peninsula was the last part of the nation of the Arabs to be affected by conflict on a larger-than-tribal scale. Except for the Hejaz, no part of the territory actually belonged to the Ottoman Empire, although the Ottomans from time to time claimed Yemen in the southwest and Kuwait on the Persian Gulf.

The British began to end the isolation of Arabia in the late nineteenth century. India was a British colony, and to get to India from Britain at that time one had to travel for three months or more by boat, through the Mediterranean and the Red Sea via the Suez Canal, along the coasts of Arabia, then across the Indian Ocean.

(61)

The ports along the Arabian coast of the Persian Gulf were the haunt of pirates, who would just as soon capture British ships as any other, particularly those loaded with goods from India. In order to protect their ships, the British made a deal with the tribal chiefs who controlled these ports, and therefore, the pirates. In return for British protection against rival tribes and an annual subsidy, the chiefs promised to cut out piracy. The system worked so well that the area became known as the "Trucial Coast" because of the truce between the British and the chiefs.

Up until the end of World War II Arabia was not involved in the struggle to form a single Arab nation. The Trucial Coast rulers were satisfied with their annual British subsidy, the British officers hired to guard them and train their bedouin tribesmen in military tactics, and their comfortable run-down palaces overlooking the sea. Oil was not a factor in their lives. Pearl diving and fishing were the only money-making activities.

Saudi Arabia and Yemen, the two territories not under British control, were hardly any better off. Oil had been discovered by Americans in the late 1930s in Saudi Arabia, and an American firm, ARAMCO (Arabian-American Oil Company), was given a concession to refine and export Saudi oil.* The main source of income then was the annual pilgrimage to Mecca. In Yemen, a mountainous land with no oil, the only products of value were coffee and qat, the leaves of a shrub that are mildly narcotic when chewed. In those days the treasurers of both countries kept the national treasury under their beds.

* Oil production did not really get underway until after World War II, when it was about 20,000 barrels a day. (Production in 1981 was 10 million barrels a day!)

The calm of Arabia was rudely shattered in the 1950s. The founder of Saudi Arabia, King Abd al-Aziz Ibn Saud, died in 1953, at about the time oil royalties were beginning to bring huge profits to his country. Because of its wealth and Islamic prestige, Saudi Arabia was drawn into the circle of Arab Muslim brotherly conflict. Its new king, Saud, was not able to manage effectively either national finances or relations with other Arab countries. In 1964 a council of leaders of the huge Saudi royal family—a tribe in itself with clans and subclans numbering thousands—deposed him for his brother, Prince Faisal (no relation of the Faisals of Iraq who belong to the Hashimite clan).

Although criticized by other Arab countries for being reactionary and a tool of the United States, Saudi Arabia under Faisal and his successors, King Khalid (1975–82) and Fahd, the present king, has not only avoided conflict with them, but also has emerged as leader of the moderate Arab governments, the ones that favor recognition of Israel and a peace settlement recognizing Palestinian rights to some sort of state that would coexist with Israel. Because of the Saudi monarchy's special position as the guardian of the holy cities, its location in the heartland of Islam and the survival of Arabian tribal society there, Saudi Arabia seemed until 1979 to have entered the modern world without losing its Islamic values or experiencing internal conflict. The extent of national economic development also seemed to rule out any violent attack on the monarchy. Ever since 1973, when oil prices were tripled, the country had been growing richer at an incredible rate. The new wealth enabled the government to guarantee for every citizen free medical care, a job, an education and a house. The divisions of the populations of other Arab nations into hostile competing groups and the failure of governments to identify with their people's wishes seemed not to be the case in Saudi Arabia.

Yet on November 20, 1979, in the middle of the annual pilgrimage, a band of armed men seized the Great Mosque in Mecca, the holiest shrine in Islam, and barricaded themselves inside. One of their leaders told the assembled pilgrims that he was the Mahdi, the "Expected One" or Messiah, who would reveal himself to the Sunni world at an appropriate time and restore the peace of Muhammad the Messenger of God. (The Sunni tradition of the Mahdi is generally similar to the Shia twelfth Imam, but it is less formal and less widely believed except by fundamentalist Muslims.)

The Saudi government spent the better part of the next two weeks trying to recapture the Great Mosque without destroying it. For much of that time they were in a state of shock. Wild rumors floated about. It was a Jewish plot against Islam, a Khomeini plot to impose Shia Islam over Arabia, a communist conspiracy. No one seemed to know who the attackers were, but every attempt to get at them was driven back with a deadly hail of gunfire. Under the mosque courtyard were three thousand hermits' cells, where pilgrims, or gunmen, could live for months on dates and milk like the early Muslims in the time of Muhammad.

The strange affair of the seizing of the Great Mosque finally ended on December 5 when the last 170 members of the band, weak from hunger and thirst, many of them wounded, surrendered to Saudi security forces. A month later sixty-three rebels were hanged in public. Most were Saudis, but other Arab countries were represented as well. As it turned out, there was no foreign plot, only Saudi and other Arab Muslims protesting the great changes that have taken place in Saudi Arabia and other Islamic lands owing to oil wealth and what they saw as the resulting corruption, decline in moral values and weakening of family bonds associated with the development of a modern nation. The Shia minority in Saudi Arabia, which has been discriminated against

(64)

as it has in other Arab countries, actually rioted in several towns in support of the mosque capture.

Saudi Arabia is a good example of the development of a pattern of violent conflict among groups that feel that for one reason or another they have been discriminated against. The discrimination takes many forms, in jobs, government positions, land distribution and educational opportunities. Discrimination against Shia is common in the Saudi state even in cases where they are competing for jobs with Sunnis and show greater aptitude for education and technical or managerial skills. As time goes on and Islamic society becomes more and more "homogenized" from the acquisition of technology, the traditional conflicts between states that are an outgrowth of the past are likely to be replaced by internal conflicts between haves and have-nots in society, with oil-producing states being more affected than non-oil producers because of their greater access to this technology and their wealth.

One possible exception to this projected pattern of internal rather than external conflict may well develop out of political ideological rivalries. In the 1970s the ruler of the oil-producing sultanate of Oman, on the east coast of Arabia, was threatened by a rebellion in Dhofar province by tribesmen who supported a rival ruler, the imam (here used as a tribal title) of Oman. The rebels were supported with arms and money by the People's Democratic Republic of Yemen (PDRY), an independent Arab state which was formerly the British crown colony of Aden. The PDRY government is Marxist in ideology and policy. The sultan of Oman is a conservative, royalist tribal leader.

As part of the shah's policy of demonstrating his intention to be the "policeman of the Gulf," he sent a battalion of regular Iranian troops plus aircraft to Oman to help the sultan put down the rebellion, which he succeeded in doing.

(65)

In addition to its conflict with Oman, the PDRY from time to time has fought border clashes with its neighbor, the Yemen Arab Republic. This conflict also represents an ideological confrontation between the Marxist PDRY and the conservative and tribal government of the Yemen Arab Republic. At the same time, however, both Yemens are committed to an eventual merger into a single Arab state, and the outcome of the conflict will determine whether that state will be an Islamic state or a Marxist state or one that is a mixture of the two ideologies. There is, however, a similarity between the kind of ideological conflicts that the two Yemens are involved in and those that may arise among the haves and have-nots within the Arab states. In both cases, the major conflict is over traditional Islam versus modern values acquired through contact with foreign cultures.

And considering the strength of the forces of traditional Islam—the Shia and fundamentalist Sunnis—this is likely to be the dominant pattern of conflict for some time in the future.

6

Syria-Lebanon: Middle of the Muddle

In the spring of 1982 one of the leaders of the state of Israel, former Defense Minister Ezer Weizman, said that in his opinion the Middle East ought to be called "the Muddle East." What he meant was that the constantly changing alliances of the Arab nations, the conflicts, the atmosphere of fear and suspicion hanging like a dark cloud over the region had created a muddle. This was a matter of great concern for the Israeli people because they were in the middle of the muddle, surrounded by Arabs who had said many times they would drive the Israelis into the sea.

A brief look at recent events involving Syria indicates how muddled things have become. In February 1982 there were violent riots in the Syrian city of Hama against the government of President Hafez al-Asad. Syria blamed the Baathist regime in Iraq. It was a natural Syrian reaction since the two Baathist regimes have been at swords' points for years. But Syria then signed a ten-year economic agreement with Iran, which was at war with Iraq. Despite Syria's enmity toward Iraq, one would have expected the Syrians not to make overtures toward Iran in view of the long-established hostility of the Iranians toward Arabs in general and Sunni Arabs in particular.

SYRIA—MANDATE TO INDEPENDENCE

Syria has always been a muddled place. Islamic Arab geographers called it al-Shams—"the Sun"—and during the great days of the caliphate it was *Mashriq*—"the East." In previous chapters we described its backward condition as an Arab province under the Ottoman Empire. A number of Arab landowning and merchant families in Syrian cities like Damascus and Aleppo cooperated with the Ottomans and were rewarded with privileges and protection. These families became an elite. When the French established their mandate, they found it to their advantage to work with leaders from these families, but not to allow any one leader to become more powerful than his rivals. Consequently, the campaign for Syrian independence was carried on by men who were jealous of each other, distrusted each other's motives, and schemed for power once the French were gone. The Syrians, like the Lebanese, had a great deal of trouble getting the French out. The last French troops did not leave until 1946, and then only under strong pressure from Britain and the United States.

Shortly thereafter the state of Israel was established in Palestine, Syria's neighbor and, in the minds of all Arabs, a part of the Arab homeland. Syrian troops, trained by the French Army, were among the Arab forces that invaded Palestine and were soundly defeated by the Israelis. The Arab defeat was a great blow to the Syrians, who had expected that the Israelis would be quickly driven into the sea.

Arab society is a "shame society" in which one group looks for mistakes that can bring shame or defeat to its rivals. On the national level, the shame comes from defeat or failure, even though foreign powers or fate can

(68)

be blamed for the failure. For Syria, the defeat was a great blow to its pride after the long and finally successful struggle for independence, and led to great instability and conflict.

The Arab defeat, the growing influence of the army officer corps and the rise of an educated middle class began in the 1950s to bring new leaders to power in Syria. The old leading families were still powerful, but their leaders could not agree on much of anything. In any case they were associated in the minds of the people with defeat, failure, the old ways of doing things that simply did not work.

For the Syrians the appeal of Arab nationalism—a single Arab nation—led to the formation of two political parties which have had a great deal to do with conflict in the country and in relation to Syria's Arab neighbors. The first party, the Syrian Social Nationalist Party (SSNP) was started in 1932 by a Christian Arab, Antun Saada. He left the country to escape the French police and went to Germany where he became a great admirer of the Nazi Party. The SSNP was organized like the Nazi Party with brown-shirt uniforms, ranks and strict discipline for the members. Saada's goal, once the French had gone, was to establish a Syrian nation which would include Syria, Palestine, Lebanon, Jordan and Iraq. The peoples of this nation, Saada said, were endowed with genius and mental abilities superior to those of their neighbors. Syria was the natural center for the new nation. The SSNP attracted a number of able young men—writers, teachers, lawyers—and seemed to be a real threat to the Syrian government established after independence. But Saada became involved in a plot to overthrow the Lebanese government and was arrested and executed by Lebanese authorities. Then in the 1950s the party was accused of supporting an American-sponsored Middle East alliance of Syria, Lebanon and other Arab nations against the Soviet Union. This was the kiss of death for most Arabs in those days because of U.S. support for Israel. Most SSNP members either dropped out of politics or joined the Baath Party.

THE SYRIAN BAATH PARTY

The Baath, or Arab Socialist Renaissance Party, which was mentioned in Chapter 5, is the dominant political party in Syria and Iraq today, and has branches in other Arab countries. The Baath Party's goal is Arab unity under its leadership, and although it has not achieved that goal, it has succeeded in maintaining power in two Arab states, Syria and Iraq.

The Baath Party was founded in 1943 by Michel Aflaq, a Christian schoolteacher who had joined the Communist Party as a student in France. Aflaq later teamed up with Salah Bitar, a Syrian Sunni Muslim, and in 1953 they joined forces with Akram Hourani, a landowner who had organized the Arab Socialist Party to help the peasants in a backward part of Syria. From then on the party was officially known as the Arab Socialist Renaissance Party, but was still called Baath.

The Baath is the first and thus far the only Arab political party in the Middle East with a definite ideology. The basic idea of Baathism, as set forth by Aflaq, is that the Arab homeland, or nation, is a single political, economic and cultural unit that will periodically go through a "renaissance" (Baath) until it meets all the needs and fulfills the dreams of the Arab people. The job of this Arab nation, led by the party, is the "reform of human existence," which means the victory over colonialism, oppression in all forms and unjust governments. Aflaq's ideas appealed to Arabs from different backgrounds, and the merger with Hourani's Socialist Party gave the Baath a touch of Islamic socialism that increased its appeal. In some respects Baathist ideology combined communism with the principles of the original community of Islam: wealth and natural resources belong to the state, and land ownership is limited to the amount a landowner can cultivate.

The goal of the party is to unify Arab society and then transform it entirely in an *inkilab*, or "overturning." The party's ideology was flexible as Aflaq and his associates developed it. As in the early days of Islam, the party recognized the existence of ethnic and religious minorities and guaranteed their separate culture and identity. Nor was there a conflict between Islam and Baathism, according to Aflaq. "Have no fear of a clash between nationalism and religion, Islam and Arabism for it is impossible; Islam in its pure truth sprang up in the heart of Arabism . . . and mixed with Arabism in its most glorious roles . . ." he wrote.

The Baath was successful not only because its ideology appealed to many Arabs, but also because of its structure. Like communist parties all over the world, the party had a tight organization, with separate units, or "cells," whose members were mostly unknown to each other. This structure enabled the party to go underground and survive during periods of oppression by Syrian governments in the 1940s and 1950s.

MILITARY COUPS

During its early years the Baath was in active opposition to successive Syrian governments. The French left no orderly political system behind when they withdrew and for many years the governments changed so quickly that it was hard to know who was in charge at any given time. The Syrian army immediately got involved in politics, often with unfortunate results. A Syrian-born American professor, who was a teen-ager at the time, remembers what it was like: "No sooner did we learn to dance to Colonel Zaim's tune, than he was executed for treason. We cheered our new hero, Colonel Sami al-Hinnawi. But he too did not last. Arab streets are filled with the debris of frustrated dreams and abandoned schemes, as each

(71)

new prophet attacks his predecessor with gay abandon."

This period of conflict among military leaders lasted five years, 1949–54. For the next few years thereafter Syrian politics was like a revolving door as military officers, civilians, Baath Party members and others chased each other in and out of power. In 1958, however, there was a sudden change. Many people began to fear that there was a communist plot to take over the country, because Soviet military and economic aid was arriving in great quantities. Also, an army general suspected of being pro-Soviet had just become commander of the armed forces. Syrian leaders looked to Egypt, the strongest Arab country, whose president, Gamal Abdel Nasser, was a popular hero among the Arabs. In January 1958 the Syrians flew to Cairo and persuaded Nasser to approve the union of Syria and Egypt into a single Arab country, the United Arab Republic.

ARAB UNITY BREAKS DOWN
The United Arab Republic (UAR) seemed to many Arabs at the time a big step toward the goal of Arab unity. Such was its appeal that the remote kingdom of Yemen, which was rapidly moving into the fourteenth century, according to a popular joke of the period, decided to join the UAR. Iraq and Jordan, not to be outdone, formed their own Union of Arab States. It lasted only long enough for the Iraqi king to be overthrown, and then collapsed. The United Arab Republic lasted barely three years before yet another dream of Arab unity fell apart. In this case it was the Syrians themselves who backed out. They felt discriminated against, because Egyptians controlled the UAR government, and Egyptian officers controlled the military. The Syrians also felt that the Egyptians considered them crude, uncultured peasants. The Syrians told Nasser that they no longer wanted to be a part of the United Arab Republic. Nasser

(72)

had to agree; he did not want Egyptians fighting their Syrian Arab brothers.

THE BAATH IN POWER
The Baath took complete control over Syria in 1963 and has been in power ever since. There have been two changes of government from that point, both involving power struggles among Baath leaders. The most important one came in 1970 as General Hafez al-Asad, Minister of Defense, took over the government. He was elected president for a seven-year term in 1971 and, as the only candidate, was re-elected in 1978.

President Asad belongs to a minority group in Syria, the Alawites, who are Shia Muslims but differ from the main body of Shia by accepting only seven Imams rather than twelve. From the time of the French mandate, the Alawite sect supplied the majority of Syrian army officers, since a military career was one of the few avenues of advancement open to them.

Up until the late 1970s President Asad was successful in maintaining order because he had the support of the Sunni majority in addition to the military. In 1978 he initiated a move to reconcile the Syrian and Iraqi Baath parties as a first step toward unification of the two countries. Union between Syria and Iraq has always seemed logical since they are neighbors, have a similar geography, climate and ethnic background. But what seems logical in the Arab world rarely turns out as expected. The union plan failed owing to bickering between the two parties over the organization of the government, and in 1980 the plan was shelved as they resumed their feud.

Iraqi Baath intrigue and resentment among the Sunni over a worsening economic situation led to internal violence in 1979–81. A number of assassinations of prominent Alawite leaders were traced to the Muslim Brotherhood. The brotherhood, founded in the 1920s, has as its goal the elimination of all present Arab-Islamic

(73)

governments in order to establish a single Islamic nation ruled by the laws of the Koran.

Efforts to suppress the brotherhood led to a "war of words" with Jordan and Iraq, whom Asad accused of harboring members after riots and a second wave of assassinations in early 1982. President Asad continues to struggle with a deteriorating economic situation and growing political opposition, but as yet there is no sign of a political organization strong enough to supplant him.

LEBANON:
FROM PEACE TO WAR

Years ago in a book entitled *Islam and the Principles of Government* an Arab writer warned his fellow Arabs against mixing religion with politics. He said that when religion interferes in government it leads inevitably to conflict, because religious groups are always hostile to each other and religious leaders divide people instead of bringing them together. Lebanon in 1982 is a perfect example of the writer's warning.

Until 1975 Lebanon was a pleasant place to live, especially for foreigners. Its capital, Beirut, was a beautiful modern city, with a dependable banking system and one of the best universities in the Muslim world. Lebanon's relationship with the French under the mandate had generally been a positive one. But beneath the surface things were not so pleasant.

Lebanon was filled with hostile religious groups crowded together in a country four-fifths the size of the state of Connecticut. If you can imagine an American state of that size in which almost every town belonged to a single group and barred its gates to outsiders, in which cities were divided into rival neighborhoods, and every male citizen carried a gun on the street, you would have an idea of what life has become for the Lebanese.

We said in earlier chapters of this book that the Maronites, an Arab Christian sect, came under European protection in the last years of the Ottoman Empire. The Maronites had moved into the mountain area of Lebanon in the seventh century to escape persecution. Over the centuries other persecuted groups moved to Mount Lebanon. The Maronites were the largest community, and during the Crusades they became affiliated with the Roman Catholic Church.

When the French took control of Lebanon, they combined the coastal region, which included Beirut, with Mount Lebanon to make up the present area of the country. This action added a large Lebanese Muslim population to the mainly Christian population of Mount Lebanon. If there can be said to be a single historical cause of the Lebanese civil war, it was the combining of Islamic and Christian groups under a single government. Before the French period the two groups were relatively autonomous, but now they became hostile to one another, and divided into warring groups within each religion.

Up until the 1970s these various groups were able to get along reasonably well in independent Lebanon. One reason for this was the Lebanese National Covenant, an unwritten agreement between the leaders of the Maronite and Sunni Muslim communities made in 1943. The covenant said that the Muslims of Lebanon would not attempt to unite the country with other Arab states, and the Christians would recognize the "Arabness" of Lebanon and not ally the country with Western Christian powers. In this way the Lebanese Christians thought they could survive as a "Christian island in an Arab Muslim sea."

The National Covenant established *confessionalism* as the basis for Lebanese political life. Confessionalism means "representation by confession," that is, each religious sect having a distinct ritual of confession and service is entitled to representation in government, the legislature and other official positions. The covenant specified that the president of the republic would be a Maronite and the prime minister a Sunni Muslim, for example. The number of seats in Parliament to which each sect was entitled depended upon its size. There are, however, many confessional sects in Lebanon plus political parties attached to several of these sects, and powerful families whose leaders are feudal lords with private armies and supporters. These differences have made it very difficult for Lebanon to become a united nation.

After 1948 a new element was introduced into the Lebanese system. When Israel became a nation about 170,000 Palestinians fled to Lebanon as refugees. Most of them were Muslims. The Lebanese Christians feared they would now drown in a Muslim sea. Lebanon did not really want the refugees since it meant almost doubling the size of the population with extra costs for food, housing and medical care. Also, having the Palestinians meant that Lebanon might become directly involved in the Arab conflict with Israel, since the Palestinian goal was to recover its homeland from the Israelis. Most of the Palestinians were housed in ramshackle refugee camps in and around Beirut. Some camps were set up in southern Lebanon where the refugees could almost see their former homes, gardens and vineyards across the border.

Palestinians in Beirut organized the Palestine Liberation Organization (PLO) in 1964, and after 1967 Lebanon as well as Jordan was a principal base for PLO guerrilla attacks on Israel. After King Hussein drove the PLO out of Jordan in 1970, Lebanon became the only remaining Arab country that allowed guerrilla attacks on Israel from its territory, mainly because the Lebanese army could not control the Palestinians. The army itself reflected the divisions of the confessional system. Sunni Muslims in the army cheered for the guerrillas; Christian soldiers, for the Israelis. The Shia, representing the lowest and least privileged religious group in the country, hoped the Israelis would destroy both Palestinians and Sunni Muslims so they would have a chance for power and wealth. These attitudes became more pronounced in the early 1970s.

THE CIVIL WAR OF 1975–76

David Gordon describes the Lebanese civil war in his book *Lebanon*: *Fragmented Nation*. It was, he writes, a war between haves and have-nots, Christians and Muslims, Lebanese nationalists and non-Lebanese Palestinians; a war between rival Arab states and ideologies on Lebanese soil and part of the confrontation between Israel and the Arabs.

The civil war began on April 13, 1975, when a busload of Palestinians passing through a Christian suburb of Beirut was shot up by Christian Maronite militiamen from the private army of Pierre Gemayel, who was then leader of the Maronite community. It ended, at least temporarily, in November 1976 when a peacekeeping army of thirty thousand Syrian troops moved into the country under the terms of a peace agreement between the various Lebanese groups arranged by other Arab nations and sponsored by Saudi Arabia. At that point the civil war had cost close to sixty thousand lives and five billion dollars in property damage.

Although the civil war officially ended with the Syrian intervention and the Saudi-sponsored peace agreement, the violence has continued. During this continuing cycle of violence Syrian troops besieged the Christian stronghold of Zahlah for three months in 1981, until a cease-fire was again arranged by Saudi Arabia. During a two-week period in May 1982 sixty persons were killed and two hundred injured in the port cities of Tyre and Sidon. Increasingly the presence of Syrian troops was seen by the Lebanese as a foreign occupation.

(77)

THE ISRAELI INVASION

It was not the Syrian presence so much as that of the Palestinians that motivated the Israeli invasion of Lebanon in June 1982. Ironically the Israeli goal was similar to King Hussein's goal in 1970—to put an end to the PLO military organization—although their long-term objectives were quite different. The Israelis defeated the Syrians in fierce fighting and drove them back to eastern Lebanon into the mountains. What was left of the PLO—perhaps five thousand to six thousand guerrillas—was bottled up in besieged west Beirut. Eventually, the PLO guerrillas were evacuated to other Arab countries, in particular to Tunisia, Algeria, and Sudan.

Yet the intensity of violence in Beirut rose again in the wake of the Israeli invasion when Lebanon's new Christian president-elect, Bashir Gemayel, was killed in a bomb attack on his headquarters in September, 1982. In response, members of a Christian militia group infiltrated the Palestinian refugee camps and murdered hundreds of Palestinian civilians. The massacre not only dramatized the continuing strife between Lebanon's Muslim and Christian communities, but also called into question the role of the Israeli army, which was responsible for preventing violence against the Palestinians.

As of this writing the Muslim Arab states have yet to develop a unified policy toward Israel in response to the Israeli invasion of Lebanon. They seem equally unable to develop either a consensus or a humanitarian policy toward the Palestinians. The real losers, however, are the Lebanese. The first generation of Lebanese young people born under independence saw their relatively peaceful existence come to an end in a hail of gunfire thirty years later. The generation born in the 1970s and 1980s has known nothing but violence.

7

Egypt: Pivotal Point of the Arab World

Egypt is the fourth largest Arab country after Sudan, Saudi Arabia and Algeria with an area of 386,100 square miles (1 million sq km), about the size of Texas and New Mexico combined. Its population in 1981 was approximately 43,876,600, nearly equal to the total population of the other Arab states of the Middle East (51,195,000). This fact alone would give Egypt a claim to leadership in the Arab world. But Egypt is an important Arab country for other reasons. Egyptians were exposed to European ideas earlier than other Arab peoples, Egypt led the Arab struggle against Israel, and Egypt has the largest number of skilled, educated people in the Arab world.

But is Egypt really an Arab nation? Other Arab nations are new, but Egypt has a 4000-year history as a separate nation. A parallel may be drawn between Egypt and Iran, for both peoples have had from their earliest history a sense of themselves as separate and individual nations, unlike the Arabs who were always a loose confederation of clans and tribes. As late as the 1940s most educated Egyptians as well as religious leaders thought the idea of Arab unity was pure fantasy. Their homeland

(79)

was Egypt; they felt that Islamic unity, not Arab unity, should be the aim of all Muslims.

Egyptians began to think of themselves seriously as "brothers" of the Arabs to the east of them after World War II. Egypt was occupied by Britain in 1882, became a British protectorate in 1914, and was under British control in one form or another until 1936. During that period the British helped develop a modern educational system, political parties, an economy based on cotton production and a regular army trained by British advisers. The British in fact gave Egypt its independence in a treaty in 1936, but kept control of the Suez Canal, the army and Egypt's foreign policy. After World War II the Egyptians saw other Arab peoples being given their independence, and this disturbed them. They identified their ruler, King Farouk, with corruption and dependence upon Britain. Anti-British feelings, along with resentment over the Arab failure against Israel, and the corrupt government of the king, came together to bring about a military coup in 1952. The coup was led by a young colonel named Gamal Abdel Nasser; his close comrade in arms was Anwar al-Sadat.

Nasser led Egypt for eighteen years (1952–70). During that period he set out to make Egypt the leader of the "Arab nation." He once said, "I have an exact knowledge of the frontiers of the Arab nation. I do not place it in the future for I think and I act as if it already existed. These frontiers end where my propaganda no longer arouses an echo."

Nasser's insistence that Egypt should play a big part in Arab unity became very popular with the Egyptian people, but it brought him into conflict with leaders of other Arab countries. His rivalry with leaders of the Syrian and the Iraqi Baath parties caused the most serious conflict. The Syrian Baath, as we said in Chapter 6, was responsible for breaking up the United Arab Republic of Egypt and Syria. Other Arab governments saw Nasser's plans as an attempt to interfere in their own affairs and overthrow these governments in the name of Arab unity.

These conflicts were mostly carried on in words, but in one case conflict led to war between Egyptians and other Arabs. This case was Yemen. As we said in Chapter 6, Yemen joined the United Arab Republic chiefly because the Imam wanted to head off Egyptian propaganda against his reactionary government. The Imams of Yemen had been in power for centuries. Their power base was the mountain tribes, but they also controlled a larger, Sunni population in the lowlands and the hot, malarial coast of the country.

A number of Yemenis went to Egypt for military training after Yemen joined the UAR, but when they returned to Yemen they were ready to overthrow the Imam, to establish a republic and begin to modernize the country. The Imam beat them to the punch by dying a natural death in 1962, so the plotters turned on his successor. They seized the Imam's palace and declared Yemen a republic. The new Imam, at first thought to be dead, turned up in the mountains where the Shia tribesmen rallied to his cause. Civil war broke out between the republican government, which was Sunni, and the Imam, backed by the Shia tribesmen.

Since Nasser had, in effect, encouraged the Yemenis to overthrow the Imam, he could hardly afford to let the new republic fall apart. He sent an army of about seventy thousand men to Yemen. The Egyptians had tanks, artillery, jet airplanes and poison gas, which they did not hesitate to use against Yemeni villages. The Yemeni tribesmen had rifles, daggers and superb knowledge of their roadless mountains. Furthermore they had the backing in arms and money of Saudi Arabia. The Saudi monarchy considered Egyptian interference in Yemen as a threat to itself. The Egyptians found that they were in over their heads in Yemen as costs and casualties mounted. The Egyptian army left Yemen in 1967, just in time to go home and be defeated by the

(81)

Israelis in the Six-Day June War. The Yemen Civil War finally ended in 1970 when with the help of Saudi Arabia an agreement was signed between the Imam's supporters and the republican government. The agreement specified that Yemen would remain an Arab republic with Shia tribal rights respected. The Imam would not be allowed to return from exile in Saudi Arabia, and at last report was living comfortably in the style of his ancestor, the Imam Hassan.

Nasser was a genius at extracting success out of failure. In 1956 the British and French invaded Egypt and routed the Egyptian army; Nasser got the United States to force them to withdraw. After Israel had defeated the Arabs in the 1967 war Nasser told the Egyptians he would resign. Millions of Egyptians poured into the streets of Cairo to reject his resignation. A generation of Egyptians had grown up under Nasser; they could not conceive of an Egyptian government without him as its leader. They called Nasser "The Boss."

For the remaining three years of his life, Nasser became more conciliatory in his relations with other Arab leaders. He mediated a number of inter-Arab disputes, and in 1970 negotiated a cease-fire between the Jordanian army and the PLO. It was his last official act; the emotional drain involved in what he himself called "racing with death to try and stop men, women and children from dying" brought on a fatal heart attack on September 28, 1970. He was fifty-two years old.

THE SADAT REGIME

Anwar al-Sadat (1918–81) was exactly Nasser's age and his closest associate. Their backgrounds were similar; both came from villages in the Nile Delta. Like Nasser, Sadat followed a military career, and the two men became acquainted during their military training. Together with a small group of other officers they organized the revolution of 1952 that overthrew King Farouk.

(82)

Sadat stayed in the background during Nasser's years in power, although he was a member of the Revolutionary Command Council and held a number of responsible positions. He stayed in Nasser's shadow, lived simply, avoided joining any political clique. It was his loyalty, dependability and apparent noncompetitiveness that probably motivated Nasser to choose him as vice-president in 1969. When Nasser died, Sadat automatically became interim president under the constitution, and in October 1970 he was formally elected president of Egypt.

Sadat had powerful rivals who felt they were better qualified than he to lead the country. Six months after his election several of them organized a plot to overthrow him. They also believed that Sadat had made a mistake to agree in April 1971 to a federation with Syria and Libya in a new Federation of Arab Republics. The federation, they felt, would weaken Egypt's leading position among the Arab states. In fact it was no more successful than other Arab attempts at union.

With his finely honed survival instinct, Sadat saw the coup coming. In May 1971 the chief plotters were arrested and sentenced to life imprisonment, but were released in 1977 under a presidential amnesty; Sadat was never a vindictive leader. From that time until his death, Sadat's authority over Egypt was not seriously challenged by any political rivals, and he became very popular with the Egyptian people.

The challenge to Sadat's leadership that developed in the late 1970s did not come from political opponents, but from fundamentalist Egyptian Muslims. They felt more and more that Sadat's programs and life style were leading Egypt away from Islam. This challenge along with the occupation of the great mosque at Mecca, Saudi Arabia, signaled a revival of activity on the part of the Muslim Brotherhood and other fundamentalist groups.

Sadat believed that he was a good Muslim and that his leadership was in accordance with the principles of

(83)

Islam. Like the shah of Iran, he was also a fatalist, a believer in *Kismet*. He felt that it was his destiny to lead Egypt. He says in his autobiography, *In Search of Identity*, "Each step I have taken over the years has been for the good of Egypt, and has been designed to serve the cause of right, liberty and peace." Sadat was convinced that his life would not end until he had achieved these goals for Egypt.

On October 6, 1976, Sadat was re-elected to a second term. A year later came his historic November 1977 journey to Jerusalem. Egypt became the first Arab state to sign a formal peace treaty with Israel. This bold action divided the Arab Islamic states. Jordan and Saudi Arabia did not take sides, Sudan supported Egypt, while others, including Algeria, Libya, Syria and Iraq, set up a "rejection front" that opposed any reconciliation with Israel, and therefore opposed Egypt as an "enemy of Arab unity and of Islam."

One might have expected that the rejectionist front would have initiated serious efforts to overthrow Sadat because of what they saw as his alleged betrayal of the Arab cause against Israel. But this did not occur, nor was there any concerted action by the rejectionist states against Israel. The normal pattern of periodic disputes, occasional moves toward union of one or more Arab states and personal rivalries among Arab leaders continued. If the Israeli-Egyptian peace treaty suggests anything in terms of Arab Islamic-state conflict, it is that other Arab states are not necessary to Egypt, but Egypt is essential to them.

On the other hand, the challenge to Sadat from Muslim fundamentalists became a tragic reality with his assassination on October 6, 1981. As he stood in the reviewing stand watching a military parade near Cairo, soldiers opened fire on him from one of the trucks in the parade. Sadat went down in a hail of bullets and died.

The soldiers who killed Sadat were Egyptians. They

were not agents of another Arab country, and there was no upheaval following his assassination. His vice-president, Hosni Mubarak, succeeded him without incident. But the fact that Egyptian Muslims assassinated Sadat is an important portent for Islamic-state conflict. As was the case in the days of the Hashishin, fundamentalist Muslims are challenging the leaders of these states to govern in accordance with the strict rules of Islam and merge their governments into one Islamic government.

Sadat's assassins declared that they were not guilty because they acted to rid Egypt of an unjust leader. He was unjust, in their opinion, because he had made peace with Israel, the enemy of Islam; he had not helped the exiled Arabs of Palestine, his blood brothers, to regain their land; and he had allowed Islam to be corrupted in Egypt by his programs to modernize Egyptian life. Lastly, they brought his own Western life style into question. Right up to the moment of their own deaths when they were hanged in a public square in Cairo, they said they were innocent of any wrongdoing.

The statements of the Egyptian soldiers strike a deep chord among Muslims. Both Sunni and Shia would like to find an Islamic alternative to Western secular government. With some exceptions, particularly among Iranian Shia, they are attracted by the economic and technological advantages, to say nothing of the higher material standards of Western society. But they do not want to give up their Islamic values, their traditional beliefs set forth fourteen hundred years ago.

As long as there are divisions within the Arab nations and divisions among the Middle Eastern Islamic nations, conflict will not be far from Muslim minds. But if we recall that day twenty-five centuries ago when Yakhdun-Lim, whom we mentioned in Chapter 1, inscribed his victory on a tablet, it seems that conflict is merely an ongoing part of Middle Eastern life, and not the controlling factor.

For Further Reading

WORKS MOSTLY ON ISLAM

Andrae, Tor. *Muhammad: The Man and His Faith*. New York: Barnes and Noble, 1935. A classic study.

Beck, Lois, and Keddie, Nikki, eds. *Women in the Muslim World*. Cambridge, Mass.: Harvard University Press, 1978.

Fernea, Elizabeth, and Bezirgan, Basima, eds. *Middle Eastern Muslim Women Speak*. Austin: University of Texas Press, 1977. Interviews with leading Muslim women, both feminists and traditionalists.

Fischer, Michael. *Iran: From Religious Dispute to Revolution*. Cambridge, MA: Harvard University Press, 1980. An excellent analysis of Shia Islam.

Guillaume, Alfred. *The Life of Muhammad*. London: Oxford University Press, 1955. Another good study.

Hitti, Philip K. *Capital Cities of Arab Islam*. Minneapolis: University of Minnesota Press, 1973. Vivid portraits of Mecca, Medina, Damascus, Baghdad, Cairo, and Cordoba.

_____. *Islam, A Way of Life*. Chicago: Henry Regnery, 1970. Well-written, straightforward discussion by one of the founders of Middle East studies.

The Koran (Qur'an). The best English translation is by A. Yusuf Ali (Indianapolis, IN: American Trust Publications). Another good one is Marmaduke Pickthall, *The Meaning of the Glorious Koran* (New York: Mentor Books/New American Library).

Rahman, Fazlur. *Islam*. New York: Holt, Rinehart & Winston, 1967.

Stewart, Desmond. *Early Islam*. New York: Time-Life Books, 1967. A book in the Time-Life Great Ages of Man series.

WORKS ON ISLAMIC POLITICS, HISTORY, ANTHROPOLOGY, AND SOCIOLOGY, EMPHASIZING CONFLICT

Bill, James, and Leiden, Carl. *Politics in the Middle East*. Boston: Little, Brown, 1974. Good chapters on "Islam and Politics" and on Islamic leaders (Nasser, Sadat, the Shah).

Dawisha, A. I. *Egypt and the Arab World*. New York: John Wiley, 1976. Good chapter on Egypt's "Arabism."

Deeb, Marius. *The Lebanese Civil War*. London: Croom Helm, 1980. Documented account of the war.

Gordon, David C. *Lebanon, The Fragmented Nation*. Stanford, CT: Hoover Institution Press, 1980. Interesting combination of civil war reportage and diary of half a century of author's life in Lebanon.

Gulick, John. *The Middle East: An Anthropological Perspective*. Pacific Palisades, CA: Goodyear Publishing, 1976. On a par with Carlton Coon's *Caravan* as a study of the underpinnings of Middle East social life.

Haim, Sylvia, ed. *Arab Nationalism: An Anthology*. Berkeley: University of California Press, 1976, 2nd edition. Original essays by Arab authors.

Holden, David, and Johns, Richard. *The House of Saud*. New York: Holt, Rinehart & Winston, 1981. Thorough study of the "family monarchy."

Hoveyda, Fereydoun. *The Fall of the Shah*. New York: Wyndham Books, 1980. The author's brother, Amir Abbas Hoveyda, was prime minister under the Shah.

Hudson, Michael. *Arab Politics: The Search for Legitimacy*. New Haven CT: Yale University Press, 1978. Especially good on Syria and Lebanon.

Lacouture, Jean. *Nasser, A Political Biography*. New York: Alfred A. Knopf, 1973.

Laffin, John. *The Arab Mind Considered*. New York: Taplinger, 1975. Interesting psychological study of Arab values and ways of thinking.

Nasser, Gamal Abdul. *Egypt's Liberation: The Philosophy of the Revolution*. Washington, DC: Public Affairs Press, 1955. One of the few books in English by an Islamic state leader.

Pahlavi, Ashraf. *Faces in a Mirror*. New York: Prentice-Hall, 1980. A book of reminiscences by the Shah's twin sister.

(87)

Pahlavi, Muhammad Reza, Shah of Iran. *Answer to History.* New York: Stein & Day, 1980. The Shah's reply to his critics.

_____. *Mission for my Country.* New York: McGraw-Hill, 1961.

el-Sadat, Anwar. *In Search of Identity: An Autobiography.* New York: Harper & Row, 1977. The life story of Egypt's late president.

Stempel, John D. *Inside the Iranian Revolution.* Bloomington: University of Indiana Press, 1981. The author is a U.S. official formerly stationed in Iran.

Stookey, Robert. *America and the Arab World: An Uneasy Encounter.* New York: John Wiley, 1975. The author was a Foreign Service officer in various Arab countries and served for many years.

Waterbury, John, and Mallakh, Ragaei. *The Middle East in the Coming Decade.* New York: McGraw-Hill, 1978.

OTHER SOURCES

Islam Centennial Fourteen—the U.S. National organization formed to celebrate the 1400th anniversary of the founding of Islam and develop better understanding of the Islamic religion among the general American public has a number of publications of interest to young readers as well. They include a packet, *Islam: An Introduction;* a booklet on Islamic science and art, *Patterns and Precision;* and *Kalila Wa Dimna,* an illustrated collection of fourteenth-century Islamic folktales.

"The World of Islam" is an excellent series of six half-hour 16-mm color films written by Exxon Educational Corporation on various aspects of traditional Islamic life, such as nomadism, architecture, calligraphy, scientific inventions, and Koranic education.

The Arab World is a series of multicultural units, with a Teacher's Handbook, prepared by Arab world consultants, with the help of librarians and elementary school teachers, for grades K–8.

Index

2012